STOP WAITING TO DIE

STOP WAITING TO DIE

A GUIDE TO MASTERING THE ART OF THE RESTART

TAMMY PACK

LIONCREST
PUBLISHING

COPYRIGHT © 2023 TAMMY PACK

STOP WAITING TO DIE
A Guide to Mastering the Art of the Restart

FIRST EDITION

ISBN		
	978-1-5445-4365-9	*Hardcover*
	978-1-5445-4366-6	*Paperback*
	978-1-5445-4367-3	*Ebook*
	978-1-5445-4368-0	*Audiobook*

To my mom in heaven, Jeannine Jordan. I wrote this book simply because it would be a crime for me to go to the grave someday, taking your wonderful teachings with me. Anything I've achieved, I owe to you. Any source of wisdom I have and have passed on to the girls is from you. Your life meant something. I love you always.

CONTENTS

INTRODUCTION

Too often, I see people around me waiting to die. Of course, they probably don't realize that's what they're doing. They think they're just plodding through life, doing the best they can. But, in fact, they have given up on the belief that it is never too late to follow your passion, fall in love, and choose a new career path. It's never too late to *live*.

When I was in my early twenties, I met a couple in their late fifties who were quite literally counting the days until they could quit their dull, unfulfilling jobs and live on social security. They had simply given up on living a life with more—a life worth actually living! While some of these people are older, most are not. Many are quite young, in fact, but they have decided it's "too late" for them to live the life they wanted. They use self-limiting beliefs to keep themselves down and, very often, to resent those who have shown the moxie to start over—those who are unwilling to accept a limited life.

Too many people sit down for way too many years, just living out their days, when they could have maximized so much more happiness in their lives. It's true that we only get one shot at life, but that shot is a lot longer than we realize.

I know a beautiful woman in her forties who, like so many of us, has gone through divorce. She has her health, her children, men clamoring to talk to her, and some money in the bank—and yet all she can think about is that she has to *start over* in her forties.

To her, I say, "Woohoo! You *get* to start over!" She *can* start over in this day and time. She has all the tools she needs to start over completely. And she is literally only middle-aged! The world is her oyster. The only thing that can hold her back is her. She will either make a restart and take over her life or sit down and wait to die.

If you are like her, you are probably putting everyone else ahead of you, which means putting yourself last. You put your kids first and live vicariously through them. We all enjoy when our kids do well, but it's all too easy to substitute your interest in them for what you're doing in your own life. Maybe you've let your health or your appearance go. Maybe you're not taking care of yourself or doing the things you know you need to do *for you*. A lot of women lose focus on themselves and struggle with taking ownership of their lives.

Or, maybe you would like to try something new—a restart on your own terms—but you think you are too old or you'll wait until after retirement. The vast majority of us are going to live for so much longer than we think. But so many people have a countdown until they can retire: "Just seven years, three months, and twenty-three days left until I can stop working and start living." What a sorry state of existence! If, when you turned sixty-five, you knew you still had thirty more years ahead of you, you wouldn't sit down and start talking about retirement—you'd start a whole new life!

Like it or not, we are all living longer, and that means we are all going to start over many times, whether in our personal or professional lives—and most likely in both.

Gone are the days when people stayed at one company for their whole working life and retired with a gold watch. You're going to have multiple careers. Depending on your age and health, when you turn sixty-five, you may move into career number three or four. Or, maybe it's not even money-making, but instead getting involved in a cause that gives you some meaning, joy, and a reason to get up every day. Maybe your restart is going back to school, finding a new relationship, or making a major move in your life.

But some of those restarts are going to be things that happen *to* you, rather than changes you decide to make—things like losing a job unexpectedly, going through a divorce, or experiencing the death of a loved one. There are all different kinds of restarts—no maximum number of them, and no minimum. They're always possible. Nothing is guaranteed in this life.

So, when something bad happens, you have two choices: you can sit down and give up, or you can keep putting one foot in front of the other and do better.

MY STORY

I do understand the temptation to give up sometimes. After all, my life was destined to be a fairy tale—until it wasn't.

I was born late in life to parents who had raised two sons but always wanted a little girl to cherish. School came easily for me, and I enjoyed it. I had an innate desire to achieve and was a Goody Two-shoes to the extreme. Even as a child, it seemed obvious to me that I would live a textbook, picket-fence, over-the-moon, happy life. I was a good kid—a really good kid—so I deserved it, right?

Yet, through a series of events—some good, some horrible—I learned the hard lesson that life is *rarely* smooth. It's almost always full of unimaginable pitfalls and hairpin turns that we cannot foresee. No one escapes this world unscathed. The differentiator between merely surviving and *thriving* is in how we handle challenges, defeats, and losses. What happens to us is often beyond our control; how we react is not. The only thing we can really do is arm ourselves with the tools to cope with what comes our way.

Learn new skills you can put in your toolbox, so that when new doors open, you can run through them and take advantage of every opportunity life has to offer. Be prepared, so that when a restart happens to you, you can get something good out of it. Build mental muscles. Know that hard seasons are coming, but you can continue pressing forward.

I recall a song about a man feeling sorry for himself when a stranger at a bar tells him, "We're still in the game." If you have breath left in you, you are still in the game! We have to choose: constantly keep pressing forward, doing our best and trying to do better; or sitting down and waiting to die.

My hope in writing this book is to share with you the tools

I have been given, and often earned the hard way, that have helped me restart my life...more times than I would like to recall.

Let's start with the day I realized I was essentially just waiting to die.

THE SIX WORDS I HAD TO HEAR

Have you ever had one sentence or one thought cause you to stop, reevaluate, and change your entire life? Of course, it's never as simple as that. There's always a backstory. But, sometimes in life, one small question and one fleeting moment can bring that backstory to the front. Hard.

I remember very well the day I heard these six probing words: "So, this is it for you?"

It was 2013, and I was walking on Main Street with my younger daughter, Sealy, who was fifteen years old at the time. We live in a charming little town where we can actually walk to Main Street from our home, stop at the candy shop, and see people we know. That day, as we walked back home, she turned to me and asked, "How old are you again, Mom?"

"I'm forty-six," I answered.

"So, I guess you've accomplished everything you want in life?" she went on. "You're happy? This is it for you?"

The look on her face told me she knew I was living my life in "good enough" mode. No major crisis at hand, no wolf at the door—but also no overwhelming joy. At that time, I owned retail stores selling women's clothing, home décor, and gifts. She knew I worked a lot—I've never minded work; in fact I have a tendency to be a workaholic—but she also knew I was married to a man, her father, who seemed to view me as a friend, a cohort, but not a wife.

He later told me that after he and Sealy had a disagreement, she told him she would forgive him if he would "treat Mom the way she deserves." Mind you, he didn't treat me badly, but the relationship wasn't what it could have been. We forget how very perceptive little eyes and ears are. Her father and I rarely fought. We just were no longer in a real relationship. And she could see it. She realized I was giving up and settling, long before I realized it—or had the energy to confront it, at least.

We all know we only have one turn "at bat" in life. We are put on earth to live once. But we constantly act as if it isn't true, don't we? We forget it every single day that we allow ourselves to drudge through a boring, stale life. I believe that settling for what we *have* because it is *way* too hard to imagine changing is a form of cowardice that sneaks up on us.

Listen, my friends: if I can summon the courage to start over—not because I wasn't successful, but because I was *not happy enough*—then you can, too.

I want to share stories from my life with you, not only to bring meaning and value to what I have both enjoyed and endured in life, but also to help you to see *yourself* in this book. Apply the lessons I have learned to *your* own story. Read every word in this book through the lens of *you*.

Wherever you are today is not where you have to be next year, and certainly not where you will be in five years. My world is *so* different from where it was just a few years ago that people who have known me for a long time often ask me, "Do you feel like you've lived two separate lives?"

To them, I say, "No, but I see your point." We only get one life, but it is a long one. It will be full of starts and restarts, and changes both good and bad. Better to live through and beyond it all than miss even a moment of that one life!

THE UNEXAMINED LIFE

Socrates said, "The unexamined life is not worth living."

Okay, I promise not to quote any more of the ancient Greeks. But think about that statement for a moment. How easy is it for us to live life just in the moment, living from one deadline to another, one crisis to another, without ever taking the time to slow down and ask, "What am I doing here? What have I learned? What can I share?"

I am as guilty as the next person when it comes to not slowing down to truly examine my life. At a conference I recently attended, my coach and friend, Tom Ferry, asked the group of high-producing realtors to ask themselves, "How many summers do I have left?"

That then led to the question, "And how do I want to spend them?"

Think about that. We are obviously not guaranteed a certain

number of summers, or days, or minutes. But how do you want to spend the ones you have? And if you're not already doing that, why not?

This book is my way of slowing down, examining my life, and sharing what I can from what I have learned and experienced.

You know the old saying, "You can't see the forest for the trees?" I often feel like I can't see the trees for the forest! By that, I mean I am so naturally inclined to look at the big picture that it is difficult for me to slow down and examine *why* I have had success, *why* I have endured so many struggles, and *how* I can encourage others who have similar struggles or who certainly will struggle in the future.

I am not much of a procrastinator in general, but there's nothing to get me moving like a good, firm deadline. Thus, I am completing my first draft of this book on the last weekend possible. My one and only six-month extension ends Monday. I haven't delayed finishing the book for lack of something to say. Goodness knows, I can always talk about something! The problem has been the ever-evolving theme of the book. *What* was I writing about? That has been my real journey. At first, I thought I would write a book about building a real estate team, since my husband and I were able to help our team skyrocket to number one in our town less than three years after going into business.

Then I spoke to some friends at a real estate conference and mentioned that I was not sure if I was on the right path with my book, and they said, "Oh, we assumed you would write about social media, since that's how you've grown your business." Picture my mental wheels turning!

They weren't wrong about that, but social media is only a channel to share information. The information, and my outlook on life, is what was underlying my success, not the channel. So then I had to look deeper at what was causing people to care what a middle-aged woman in a small town in Texas had to say on social media. What lessons or convictions was I sharing that reached people? I knew if I dug deeper, there was much more I could say to help those who were struggling, looking for hope, and looking for someone to remind them that their only source of happiness and success was—to a great degree—in their own hands.

Working on the title of the book gave me the most clarity of all. At the end of the day, every lesson I was trying to magnify, and every story I was hoping to share, had one true kernel in common: they all focused on the art of the restart. Looking back over my fifty-five years, I realized that life has been one restart after the other—in business, in relationships, and in my own health and wellness journey.

And that concept of restarting is universal to all of us.

We all either choose to restart or sit down and basically "wait to die." I'm sure this is rarely a conscious thought, but rather a *lack* of thought. I have known people of *all* ages who decided that where they were in life was as good as it was going to get. How sad! And in this amazing day and age…how utterly unnecessary!

I'm not going to begin to tell you I have every answer. What I *can* tell you is that I look younger—or at least better—than I did ten years ago. I smile more than I ever have, and I have meaningful relationships with more people in more places than I *ever* could have dreamed.

Sounds good, right? But why did this happen? How did I do it? Can others do this, too? I hope I can tell you. I am going to try. Because everyone deserves to be as happy and as successful as they possibly can be.

It is going to be hard; I'm not going to lie to you and tell you that it won't be. But I hope by sharing *all* of my restarts—the good, bad, and ugly—and what led to them, how I got through them, and how I learned there's always another one coming, you can find similar success, personally and professionally, as you move through your own inevitable changes.

This doesn't just apply to people who are over the age of fifty. I talk to young people all the time and tell them, "Quit worrying so much about where you start, because that's not where you're going to end up. You're going to keep moving up—unless you're too afraid to even get in the starting blocks." I think this paralysis among young people has become an epidemic. Because of social media, they are able to see people who "have it all." And they try to figure out how *they* can have it all. That is a question that simply cannot be answered at that age. The most important thing at that age is simply to start. Exceed expectations in everything you do and let the restarts come when they may.

Whether you are just getting started or facing yet another restart, and whether you are in your twenties or approaching retirement, you can learn from the experiences of others so you'll be able to go through your next restart and come out the other side better than ever.

You *are* going to have restarts, no matter who you are. It's impossible to know exactly when sometimes, but they're coming. If you're blessed to live long enough, then you're going to have to restart—and, very likely, not just once.

I got stuck with my first restart pretty early: a divorce at age twenty-four. But before we talk about that first, extremely unexpected restart, I want to rewind a bit and show you how I got there.

CHAPTER 1

═══

AN EARLY EDUCATION

Six weeks into the second grade, my mom sat me on the kitchen counter, cupped the back of my head in her hand over the sink, and washed my hair. Boy, did I hate that routine! Usually, I would delay it as long as possible. But this day was different. My mom clearly had something on her mind that she wanted to discuss while we went through this despised ritual.

She was trying to be sensitive, I think, and not upset me when she casually threw out, "The school called and wanted to know if you wanted to go ahead and move up to third grade."

A normal kid might worry about their friends or how the change would affect their playtime at recess, so she was approaching the topic carefully. But I immediately said, "Well, yes, of course!"

Even at age seven, I couldn't comprehend why anyone would turn down an opportunity to advance! If I had the chance to leave behind those suckers in my class, why wouldn't I?

So, I made the move up, and it went very smoothly—well, as smoothly as it could in the east Texas public school I attended.

As the years went by, however, my mother noticed I was allowing myself to coast. I was slipping into comfortable mediocrity, and that was *never* going to be okay with my mom. In sixth grade, I had a "C" on a report card and made the laughable excuse that many of us have probably used over the years: "But Mom, a C isn't bad; it's *average!*"

My mother never insisted I make straight A's or any other academic standard. But she did insist throughout my entire life that I always do *my best*. Boy, that puts the pressure on, doesn't it? She could see I was performing down to the level of those around me—and down to the expectations, however low they were, that my teachers had of me. Something had to be done.

So, in the middle of my sixth-grade year, I changed schools and moved over to a private Christian school in Shreveport, Louisiana, about forty miles from where we lived. My cousin who lived in Shreveport went there, so it was on the radar. But, as luck would have it, they didn't have room for me in their sixth-grade class. I was really excited about the transfer, so not to be deterred and to avoid the waiting list, I just went back to fifth grade where they had an opening. I really didn't mind at all since my cousin was also in fifth grade. We were the same age, so she was in our "correct" grade.

However, as I got into high school, it bugged me that I had lost that year of getting ahead! So as I started my junior year of high school, I looked at the credits required to graduate and learned that I would need only 1.5 credits in my *entire* senior year, mostly because I had taken some classes in summer school. I mean, who goes to summer school for fun? This girl.

Summer school in high school is usually remedial, but thanks to a government initiative through the state of Louisiana, our school was able to offer a Gifted and Talented summer program. They only offered classes during that one summer on computer science and statistics, but—nerd that I was—I said, "Sure! I would love to drive forty miles each way, all summer long, to take classes that don't really get me anywhere!"

The fact that I had taken those summer school classes for fun really paid off when I learned I could take the remaining 1.5 credits I needed via correspondence course during my junior year, thereby graduating high school a year early.

I'm here to tell you those correspondence courses were *way* harder than my normal high school classes! I was technically valedictorian of the senior class, even though I was not even part of the senior class when I graduated. They recognized the kid who would have been valedictorian instead of me, as they should have, but that title did get me some college scholarship money. The fact that there were only a dozen students in that graduating class didn't keep me from receiving the scholarship!

MY INTERNAL DRIVE

Looking back over my life, I believe the internal drive to succeed was built into my genetic makeup. I know we all have the *ability* to succeed, but I also believe that—like most things—drive comes more naturally to some than to others.

So perhaps we should start with an assessment. On a one-to-ten scale, how would you rate your internal drive? Your competitive edge? If you're a two, could you become an eight? I don't know. Just being perfectly honest, I've never lacked the drive to achieve or to win, so I have no idea if it can be acquired. But I'm betting most of you do have a strong desire to achieve and to do better. Maybe you just need to reignite the old competitive fire and believe in yourself again.

It can be tempting to focus on doing just what it takes to get by and no more. Have you ever heard the expression, "Bosses pay just enough so employees won't quit, and employees do just enough not to get fired?" That's a guaranteed prescription for mediocrity and is certain to lead to an unfulfilled life. Just getting by, just doing the minimum, is the absolute definition of sitting down and waiting to die. Life is to be *lived*, not endured.

I always wanted to be the best at whatever I was doing. I wasn't always the best, but I at least had the desire.

And I had to find what I was good at. I was not good at sports, so I didn't try to be the best at that; it would have taken a lot of effort just to go nowhere. But I was good at school, so that's what I focused on.

I guess I always had a competitive spirit, an internal drive to be number one at something. Now, let's be clear: I have zero athletic skills! In PE class, my best friend and I would typically be the first to allow ourselves to be captured in Capture the Flag so we could sit and chat. We would also lag behind the pack if we were running—and I use that word *very* loosely—laps around the track.

She never let me forget the time when we were pulling up the rear as usual—the extreme rear, let me be clear again—and, for some strange reason, as we headed into the home stretch, I suddenly mustered what tiny bit of speed I had and raced across the finish line without her. What kind of friend does that?

I think I mumbled something to the effect that I just assumed at the end of the race we would kick it in gear and make a run for the finish line. I had no desire to embarrass her. I just had some little piece of DNA in me that made it feel obvious that when the chips are down, you do what it takes to pull ahead. That is not a moment I am proud of, but if I could go back and change it, all I would do differently would be to play fair by giving her a warning that I was going to go all out for the last stretch. Then she could have decided if she wanted to join. I'm quite sure she would've said, "Knock yourself out!"

To this day, people ask me where I get my motivation and drive. I probably seem bumfuzzled, looking at them like, "How do you *not* have motivation and drive?" In all areas of academia, and later in business, I have naturally wanted to get to the top and do it faster than anyone else. I couldn't run fast—but I was always in a hurry, as long as it didn't require breaking a sweat.

NATURALLY COMPETITIVE

Let's be clear about something else: life in high school was no picnic for an egghead like me. I tried out for cheerleading several times and never made it. I was too uncoordinated, too awkward, and not nearly popular enough to be voted in by the student body. My hair was "mean," as my mom liked to call it. I had a gap in my front teeth and an annoying propensity for letting my classmates know that I knew more than they did (or, at least I thought I did).

Like most kids in high school, I felt completely pigeonholed and was ready to move on to the next phase. A teacher once told our high school class to enjoy every moment, since these were the best years of our lives. My equally dorky best friend looked over at me and whispered, "Then the future's looking mighty dim!"

We both exemplified the concept of late bloomers!

Luckily, that teacher could not have been more wrong! Those were some of the most boring, frustrating years of my life, and I was thrilled to get out of there a year ahead of schedule.

I was the first person in my family to attend a full, four-year college. Like most people, I didn't really know what I was doing as I prepared for college. But I *was* voted Most Studious in high school, so I did what I do best: I studied.

Back then, we planned our courses from a paper catalog sent by the college in the mail, intended to help us decide on a major. We didn't have the internet to help us find every course with the click of a button. Sometimes, I miss the ability to highlight, underline, and fold down page corners while making a decision about some great life event, whether it was what my major would be in college or which magnificent Barbie accessories I would ask Santa to bring me from the Sears catalog as a child! In fact, I still have that college catalog, which was already dog-eared and marked up long before I arrived on campus at Abilene Christian University (ACU) that summer.

Abilene Christian is a university affiliated with the Church of Christ, which I had attended all my life. Friends of my church had gone to ACU. My first boyfriend was currently attending ACU. Where else would I have gone? In those days, our options were few, but we were happy to have options at all. There was no internet—no way of looking for opportunities the way we can today. I do recall receiving mailers from the military academies, but since I couldn't do a single push-up, I was pretty sure I was not qualified!

In the early eighties, when I started college, we didn't register online. We showed up to college and *then* met with an advisor to help us enroll in the needed classes. At the appointed time for freshman registration, I walked into the counselor's office and said, "Is there a rule that you have to go to college for four years? Because using this catalog, I've put together a two-and-a-half-year plan, and a three-year plan as a backup. I can't possibly see how this could take four years!"

The counselor looked at my drafted plans, grinned from ear to ear, and said, "You'll be fine. You don't need my help with this. Next!"

I believe most people would look at the same situation and think, *This is the plan laid out by the school. How much work do I need to do to succeed, or at least to get by?*

Something inside me just propels me to want to go faster or look for a better, more efficient way. Why? Because I know I can get more done in the same amount of time.

A CHANGE OF PLANS

Although my two-and-a-half-year plan proved a little ambitious, I was able to graduate summa cum laude, with a 3.87 GPA and a degree in government, in three years.

I accomplished this by using a mixture of strategies. First, I was able to test out of nine hours of credits before starting college. I tested out of the full year of freshman English, plus a required Bible course called Life and Teachings of Christ—which, without a doubt, was the most difficult test I have ever taken. ACU would prefer you take your Bible classes *there*, so they do not make it easy to get out of them!

Then, the summer after my freshman year, I was accepted into a six-week program at Georgetown University in Washington, DC, called the Institute for Comparative Political and Economic Systems. Nerds. Our group of roughly one hundred college students selected from around the country took two classes at Georgetown in the mornings: one on political systems, and one on economic systems. Then, in the afternoons, we had the opportunity to work on Capitol Hill in internships arranged for us by the Institute.

I was lucky to be assigned to work for then-Senator Phil Gramm, a Republican from Texas. I pictured a senator working in an office with maybe four or five assistants—so imagine my astonishment to see that his staff of approximately fifty aides took up an *entire wing* of the Russell Senate Building! This certainly was no internship where you worked closely with the senator, sitting in a small office, pontificating over foreign policy.

I have to say that six-week internship caused me to become very jaded when it comes to politics. The other interns, junior aides, and I were assigned the mission of answering constituents' letters. You know how you are always being urged to "write your congressman?" Well, I can tell you that your letter is read and answered by some wet-behind-the-ears college kid who writes back telling you what you want to hear. I quickly figured out that the senator wasn't particularly interested in what was in those letters. His stance was that he was elected on a particular platform, and, based on his own decision-making ability, he felt completely comfortable voting as he saw fit. Ever the realist, I didn't take offense at the situation. I just realized what I was doing was basically a waste of time. And we've already discussed how much I enjoy wasting time!

I also looked around while I was there and realized that the full-time administrative assistants' wages were horrible, especially considering that they had to live in super pricey Washington, DC! The only staffers making a decent wage at all, which I believe was around $60,000 in 1985, were those with law degrees. So, I decided right then that a law degree was probably in my future. That way, I could either practice law or work in politics with at least some hope of being able to pay the bills.

Stop and think about the career and life choices available to you at this very moment. Are you realistically evaluating as you go along? Are you considering whether you will be able to sustain yourself and your family in the way you would like? If not, are there deviations or detours you can make that will increase your odds of future success? I have had numerous college students, beyond my own children, ask me what they should study, where they should study, and what books they should read. So few people end up working directly in their field of study for more than a few years, and so rarely will the school you attend make a huge difference in your life.

My advice is usually the same: stop stressing about it, do your best, and enjoy the process! Your main job when you're young—and throughout *life*—is to pursue courses and paths that leave as many doors open to you as possible. When you do that, then you give yourself more chances to walk through them. Always choose the path that offers another fork in the road down the way. Make every decision in a way that will maximize your ability to make choices and be nimble. Because whatever you think you're going to be doing as a grownup, and even if you're fifty, is likely not what you will be doing in a decade.

I went to law school thinking that if I still ended up deciding to work for the government, at least I would be in Washington—with one of the higher-paid jobs—or I could opt to be a prosecutor, work in the private sector, or work for a corporation. The choice to go to law school was a way of opening as many doors as possible.

GOING ABROAD

In the summer after my second year of college, I took a full course load of fifteen hours at the local college, East Texas Baptist University—which was a breeze after spending the previous summer at Georgetown!

When I went back to ACU for my third and final year, I spent the first semester studying abroad.

Abilene Christian didn't offer study abroad, though, so this was an opportunity that few students there pursued. Once again, I had to rely on my internal drive and go on the search without the benefit of Google! I discovered that our sister school—Harding University in Searcy, Arkansas—had a program in Florence, Italy. I applied and was accepted, so I headed off once again to meet college kids who knew each other but were strangers to me.

Studying abroad in Italy sounds so high-class—but, in reality, the cheapest time you will *ever* be able to spend abroad is when you are in school. The tuition is the same, and so is the room and board. The only extra costs are the flights there and back and some spending money for tours.

One complicating factor of my study-abroad program on my three-year plan was that 1984, when I started college, was the first year ACU introduced a new honors program. I was invited to be on the student cabinet, acting as a liaison while the details of the new program were fleshed out.

There were only a few honors courses offered, which made it tough to get all thirty honors hours that were needed to graduate with University Honors. It was even tougher when I compressed my time down to three years, and tougher still when one of those semesters was abroad at a different university!

When it was time to graduate, I found I needed *one* more class to qualify for the honors program. Never one to be deterred, I thought about which of the courses I had taken abroad might possibly qualify as honors level. I went to the head of the ACU Bible department and showed him that I had taken Life and Teachings of Paul while in Italy. During that course, we had visited many of Paul's stops in Italy and traveled to Greece, where we read his Acts 17 speech from the top of Mars Hill while *we* were at Mars Hill. I argued that if that didn't make that Bible class honors level, then I didn't know what would. Luckily, I won him over and received the final three hours I needed to have the honorific "with University Honors" added to my diploma.

Most people tend to give up very easily. At the first obstacle, they throw up their hands and start complaining. If your argument is just and right, however, there is usually someone out there who is willing and able to help you—if you treat them with respect and kindness.

After returning from Florence, I had just one semester left before graduation. The workload required to finish on time that final semester was *awful*. I had to take fifteen hours of all upper-level government classes with writing requirements and—wait for it—*golf*. ACU required four, one-hour physical education classes—and you know how much I love those. I went to every class and made A's on all the tests, but I could only hit the ball about 50 percent of the time. It never seemed right to me that my GPA could be affected by my already-noted lack of physical prowess. Frankly, I'm still bitter.

I moved past it and wrapped up my undergraduate studies, turning twenty just a few weeks before graduation, but I still looked twelve years old. My mom told me, "You look so young, no one's going to want to hire you; you need to get some more schooling."

So, in an example of positive rationalization, I told myself, "Well,

I graduated high school a year early and college a year early. Law school is three years. So it will basically cost me one total year. Not too bad!"

And off to law school I went.

CHAPTER 2

======

CAREER ASPIRATIONS

After I graduated from high school, I had a whole summer with nothing to do. It seemed like a good idea to get a job, which was something new for me. Why not earn a little cash, right? So I drove down to Marshall Mall. Remember when the mall was *the* place to be?

Typical of many small towns, our mall was a pretty depressing sight with so few stores still in business. There was the ubiquitous Orange Julius, a JC Penney, and a chocolate shop (which my dad always remarked sold chocolate for "a dollar a bite.") Of the slim pickings available, my top choice for potential employment was Stuart's, a clothing store where most of the girls my age shopped. I walked up to the counter, palms sweating, and asked for an application. The professionally-dressed woman behind the counter seemed a bit frazzled but pulled out a blank application and handed it to me, albeit in a distracted and disinterested manner. She barely made eye contact and clearly had bigger fish to fry at that moment than speaking with yet another fresh-faced kid looking to enter the high-stakes world of retail sales down at the local mall.

My heart sank as I glanced at the stack of completed applications on the counter, at least an inch thick. I began filling out my application, my head spinning trying to think of a way to distinguish myself from the pile of what I was sure were more qualified candidates. My mother had told me it would be hard for me to find work at the mall (she had the benefit of knowing I had zero experience and no real qualifications at all)—and, let's face it, everyone wanted that one lone job! I surely did not want to prove my mom right.

I noticed I had put some information in the wrong blank—in pen—so I had to decide quickly whether to scratch through the mistake (would this make me look sloppy?) or ask for a fresh application. After seeing my opportunity, I casually said, "Could I please have another application? You would *think* a valedictorian could fill this form out correctly!"

The woman stopped in her tracks. "You're valedictorian?"

Of course there was no reason to go into the fact that there were only twelve people in my entire graduating class—or that I didn't *technically* win the title, since I had skipped a grade. The point was I would certainly be smart and hard-working enough to sort and hang clothes and check out customers at Marshall Mall. She offered me the job on the spot! Had I kept to myself, quietly filling out my application so it could be added to that dusty stack, I doubt seriously that I would have landed that first, ever-so-important job.

Just a small amount of self-promotion, done in the right manner, can go a long way!

SELF-PROMOTION

Did you read that right? Am I suggesting that you promote yourself? Absolutely! My mom always told me, "You have to speak up to be noticed."

I know and work with a lot of individuals—usually women—who struggle mightily with self-promotion. By "self-promotion," I mean being willing to showcase your talents in the right way and at the right time, and being willing to speak up confidently about things you are good at. It just *feels* wrong to many women.

I can't say it came naturally to me, either, because it certainly did not! But I saw the value pretty early on. Most people are surprised to learn I was very shy as a child and would try to stand behind my mom when she was talking to someone. From a young age, she would pull me out and insist that I look them in the eye and smile; you know, be normal! It took effort on her part, but she slowly and consistently helped me overcome my shyness, or most of it, so I could be noticed and advance my position as well as help others.

There are many benefits of self-promotion when it is done correctly. You will be on the radar of teachers, clients, even people you would like to help. But to really pull this off, you need to possess a high EQ (emotional quotient), whether inherited, developed, or both. Most things in life are about balance. In an educational setting, don't be afraid to contribute, to raise your hand, or to share an answer. On the other hand, don't be that person who gives every answer and always wants to be heard. It's all about give and take. I've learned that most people find it easier to sit back and not promote what they know or can do at all. That puts them in high danger of simply being overlooked.

So I have this nailed down, right? Of course not. We are all works in progress. I have a weekly Zoom call with about fifty high-level eXp Realty agents, and I've noticed I don't speak up very often. So, guess what? When speaking opportunities come up, I'm not first on anyone's mind, though I feel I can do as good a job as any of them—even better than most. Why should they notice me if I don't put myself out there? As with most things in life that are worthwhile, it takes courage.

It's hard to help anyone, including yourself, if you are invisible. And if you aren't willing to speak up for yourself, you will certainly miss some great opportunities in life. It can be hard at first, but it can be done in baby steps. I don't have to go from saying nothing on those Zoom calls to running the agenda. That would be super annoying. What I can do is make one comment. Maybe give a compliment to the group or to someone for a job well done. Start with something low-risk and build up your tolerance. The feedback you receive will nearly always be positive, and you will soon be wondering why on earth you weren't speaking up all along.

NEVER FORGET HUMILITY

Self-promotion and humility are not mutually exclusive. Even if it was a bit of a ploy, I used the self-promotion of mentioning that I was valedictorian in a self-deprecating way. Pointing out my mistake of putting my name in the wrong blank showed I knew I was fallible and was willing to admit mistakes. Letting people know you are capable, interested, and willing is extremely important. But so is letting them know you are humble, eager to learn, and coachable. No boss is looking to hire a know-it-all.

Sometimes, people play down their gifts as a way of seeking attention. Have you ever witnessed this? When my daughter, Sealy, was in elementary school, she would come home so annoyed that one of the girls in class would say her art project was terrible while knowing full well it was the best one. Nothing is more frustrating than watching someone sell themselves short so others will brag on them. So needy!

If you've ever given into the temptation, let's just put an end to that. People are aware of what is happening, and it makes you appear less than genuine. Take the skills and gifts you have—and we *all* have some—and own them in a confident, yet humble way. (No, that is not an oxymoron!)

MY LESSON IN HUMILITY

As it turned out, the woman who hired me that summer was a district manager filling in temporarily while they looked for a new manager. They soon found one, and as luck would have it, it was someone I had known from church in my younger days. She didn't attend that often, but I knew her, and she knew me.

We all tend to judge people by what little we can observe on the surface. She had observed me as "the golden child" of my parents, and she wasn't entirely wrong. Based solely on the fact that my parents doted on me, she decided I was likely spoiled and lazy. Not a bad bet in general, but I wasn't. Now, as Mom would say, I was always "more mental than physical," but I did the job I was there to do.

I may have been my parents' "golden child," but I was also a product of their depression-era work ethic. Neither of my parents cursed at all, but the absolute worst four-letter word you could be called in my family was L-A-Z-Y.

On my first day at the new job with this woman as my new manager, she asked me to take the trash cans from the bathrooms and go out back to wash them out with the water hose. No problem. You get a job; you do what you're told. I did that task and several others, but as it turns out, she was testing me. I later learned, to my disbelief, she actually expected me to refuse. I was so proud when that summer came to an end and she told my mom that she thought I would be spoiled and not want to do any of the "dirty work," but she was wrong. She told my mom I was very sweet and always willing to do whatever needed to be done. I guess she didn't realize who raised me! Nevertheless, it made my mom proud. And nothing ever made me happier than making my mom proud.

Years later, my daughter Sealy was sitting across from me at my desk during a visit home from college. She looked at me in astonishment as my phone rang, my computer popped up messages, various agents poked their heads in the door to ask me questions—you know, just the typical life of a leader in a business—and then my assistant walked by and said, "The toilet is clogged. I'll call the plumber."

What does a leader do in that situation? Grab a plunger!

Sealy said, "Gross! Why do you have to do it?"

"Who else do *you* think should do it?" I asked her in response. "You can't be a leader by asking people to do what you aren't willing to do."

We teach others by example. If I am "too good" to pick up a plunger, then I have just taught everyone in my organization that they should be—or aspire to be—"too good," as well. And that's not the way to create and foster a healthy culture in the office or in the home.

All types of hard work are honorable. As they used to say back home, "I don't have any heartburn with anyone making an honest living." You may also remember hearing, "Don't get above your raisin'." Even the Bible admonishes us not to think more highly of ourselves than we should. You *must* lead by example.

And, for goodness' sake, don't be afraid to get your hands dirty.

LAW SCHOOL KICKS MY BUTT

I wasn't one of those people who had a burning desire to be an attorney from an early age, so I thought, *I'll take the LSAT, and if it goes well, I'll go to law school.*

With no prep at all, I did well enough on the test, so I applied to four or five schools. I was fortunate to get into the University of Texas School of Law—a Top Fifteen law school. I also got into the University of Alabama Law School and went to meet with the counselor there. I'll never forget the man telling me, "We'll be happy to give you a scholarship. But you got into UT Law School. You really have to go there."

So, I did.

Well, let me tell you, Miss Valedictorian got her butt kicked.

Being in law school was nothing like undergraduate studies! For one thing, I was barely twenty years old, and many students in my class had already spent time out in the "real world" after earning their bachelor's, working as investment bankers and in other job titles I barely recognized. Secondly, UT grades on a true bell curve, which means that a certain percent of students should make A's, and a similar percent should fail. I can't tell you how ridiculous I found this notion, given how difficult it is to *get into* UT Law School. The year I started, only one in seven applicants was admitted, but a certain percent of those should fail? This caused a culture of extreme competition, as you can imagine.

On one of my first days, I pulled up my lunch tray, loaded with a huge, stuffed baked potato, Diet Coke, and Snickers bar, to a table of classmates in the student center. They looked at me awkwardly, and then one of them broke it to me: "This is our study group, and we are working together on our outlines for Civil Procedure." I acted like it didn't bother me not to be included, picked up my tray, and slinked off to another table far, far away. That's when I realized I definitely was not in Kansas anymore!

So, what did I do? Well, I buckled down, did what I needed to do, and graduated in roughly the top 40 percent of my class. That sounds low until I remember how impressive every single student in my class was!

As with every part of life, it was time to restart. High school, and even college, had been relatively easy. Now, I had to restart my thought process on school in general, on taking notes, and on creating disciplined study routines. I had to shift most of my focus from memorization and rote recitation to critical thinking and effective writing.

When lifting weights, the goal is to break down the muscle over and over so it heals stronger. That's a good metaphor for my law school experience—and for life, too. We either allow the world and outside forces to break us down to our destruction, or we break ourselves down so we can continually heal and become stronger in every area of our lives. Restarting my academic career in law school was one of the most difficult, humbling things I have ever done. However, it taught me so much more than how to search for legal precedent or write a compelling argument. It taught me that life would not always be easy, *even for me*, and only I could do something about it!

LEARNING TO TRUST MY VOICE

One of the few law school memories that really stands out for me is the moment where I found the confidence to follow my gut and embrace my own unique presentation style and speaking voice. Law schools offer two extracurricular scholastic competitions known as mock trial and moot court. Mock trial simulates a trial in the format most of us are familiar with—calling witnesses, making opening and closing statements, and arguing cases. Moot court is an appellate competition where you simulate presenting your case to an appellate court after a verdict has already been rendered by the trial court.

In either competition, we were given a packet which included the set of facts of our case. The cases were carefully crafted to be evenly weighted for both sides—for example, assuming the case was criminal, roughly 50 percent of the evidence made the defendant look guilty and 50 percent made him look innocent. To increase the challenge, we were randomly assigned to represent the defendant or the state (prosecution) one week, and then, if we advanced, we would represent the opposite side the next week.

I found both competitions very useful in forming the thought process that I use to this day. If I can pinpoint anything that has made me even-keeled (even to the point of being annoyingly detached from outcomes sometimes) and willing to see things from another perspective, it is this experience.

Since it was a competition, I naturally became very passionate about my side of the case. But the following week, I would be required to do an about-face and go against everything I had just defended so passionately. The lesson learned? Every story has two sides. And two sides can both be equally correct given the paradigm through which you see the situation. Always make sure you know and *acknowledge* both sides. *Always.* The moment I can see you are a "one side has all the answers" person, I may love you, but I no longer respect your opinion. No one but God Almighty has a monopoly on truth.

For the big moot court competition, I went to the school office to sign up for a partner. I mostly socialized with friends from church rather than my law school colleagues, so getting a "potluck" partner would have to suffice.

I was assigned to a young man from New York, and we were about as different as night and day. He was a short fellow, about my size, but very confident—even cocky. He spoke in his fast, clipped New York accent. I spoke in my Southern accent, which

I could describe poetically as more of a slow drawl, but if you've ever heard me talk, you know I speak faster than any Yankee you could ever meet!

We got together and worked on our strategy. We also attended a demonstration put on by the previous year's winners. I was impressed that these young people had won last year's competition amid a very strong field of future rock-star attorneys. I also distinctly remember thinking, *Boy, are they rigid and rehearsed! Is this really what we're supposed to do?*

Yes, apparently that's what we were supposed to do. I mean, they won, after all! My first thought was, *I never want to seem so plastic and stiff.* But then again, what could I possibly know at age twenty that the University of Texas Law School champs didn't know?

So, I went into our first competition nervous as can be, with sweaty palms, racing heartbeat, and a churning feeling in my stomach. I stood up there in my best gray suit jacket with a matching skirt and my red bow tie (ladies' version, but still, what were we thinking?), and I began mimicking what last year's winners had done. I made my presentation in the most stiff, judicial voice and posture you can imagine. My hands were flat on the podium, my head turning side to side slowly like a robot acknowledging each of the judges. No emotion, just facts. It was not me. It was not my wheelhouse. It did not go well.

We received our scores after that first round. My partner's score was in the nineties, and mine was in the seventies. On the strength of his score, we had eked out a victory and moved on to the next round. Well, that was the epitome of humiliation and just wasn't going to work for me! I thought to myself, *Forget it! Being stiff looks ridiculous to me when I watch other people do it, so I'm done with that. I'm going to be myself and talk like a normal person. And if that's not what they want, so be it. Clearly the stiff thing isn't working out.*

If I was going down in flames, I was going down as *me!*

As upset as I was with my score, my partner seemed pretty okay with it. He enjoyed telling me how to improve. I can't really blame him since my score stunk! But I didn't like it; I felt that he was unbelievably condescending, even when I assured him I knew where I went wrong and was prepared to correct my course.

And correct it I did.

Speaking in public in a confident and relaxed style requires a lot of mental discipline. It's one of those things that is hard to make look easy. In fact, this was probably the second time in my early life where I have a clear memory of *choosing* to control my mindset—and both times centered on public speaking.

The first time was when I was a freshman at ACU. In my first semester, I signed up for Freshman Speech (Honors version). I had never taken a speech class before, and—like almost every human being—I was very scared to stand in front of the class and deliver a presentation. As I prepared for the speech, I went deeply inward for inspiration on how to not only write and deliver a good speech but also feel relaxed while doing it. I thought, *How do I feel when I'm watching someone else give a speech? Am I hoping they fail? Or am I cheering them on?* Even if not being particularly altruistic, I realized my *personal* comfort level is much higher when watching a confident speaker than one who is fumbling, stuttering, and sweating. I realized they are just like me; they *want* me to do well for *their own* peace of mind!

Watching others who were relaxed and seemed to be having fun made *me* feel relaxed, as well. Those who were nervous made me nervous. So, whether I was sweaty and made a fool of myself or just spoke from the heart and had fun...either way, I had to do it, so I might as well do my best to have a good time!

I decided to force myself mentally to relax and speak naturally, the way I would if I were having a conversation with just one person. And it worked! My ACU speech professor actually encouraged me to change my major to speech after that. I laughed and thought, *How do you ever get a job making speeches?* Ironically, I've pretty much been doing that in one form or another since that day.

Back to my moot court competition: I decided to control my mindset and speak naturally, just the way I had in that Honors Speech class. I had tried to follow what everyone else did, but it felt plastic and wrong. That was my mistake. I had to at least *try* doing it the way I felt it should be done—the way I'd want someone to talk to me if I were a judge or jury. You don't want to be bored stiff listening to a case that could be a matter of life or death!

I trusted who I was and what I thought was right, and I made my speech more interesting, in my own voice. And my scores shot into the nineties!

Unfortunately, I believe my sudden success caused my partner to feel insecure, and his scores dropped into the seventies. Suddenly, *I* was the one carrying the team, and *he* was the dead weight! Despite his increased fumbling and bumbling, I was able to carry us to the quarterfinals before we were defeated—a feat I am proud of to this day, given the extreme competition. The power of a correct mindset!

A lot of people say you need to find your voice, but I had to learn to *trust* mine. I had to trust that what felt normal to me was what I needed to do. Nobody in that preparation room would have told me to just go with my own folksy style, but that's what worked for me. I had nothing to lose by trusting myself, because doing things the same way as those other people was clearly not going to work.

That's something you can learn, too. We're all taught from a young age to follow the rules, respect what we're taught, and do what the experts or authorities tell us to do. But there's a point where you do have to trust yourself and trust what you know to be right.

I'd learned that lesson well in law school, but trusting my gut when something just wasn't right was a lesson I'd have to learn more than once.

CHAPTER 3

MY FIRST SERIOUS RESTART

Before we start down this difficult path, I feel I should share with you the one thing about writing this book that has given me the most trepidation: how to deal with the stories surrounding my two ex-husbands. Yes, that's a bit of a spoiler alert. But I think it is essential that you understand my thought process here. I have not used either of their names. I didn't think it was necessary; and making up fake names just felt silly.

My exes are not bad guys. They're just guys. Just humans, flawed as we all are. Did they do some lousy things to me? Well, I think so. But they aren't here to respond and give their opinions. I have no doubt many of you who are in long, happy marriages have had similar (or worse) things happen between you. Just remember these are my opinions, my interpretations, and my feelings about those years and those incidents. I wish I could leave them out altogether, but they are simply too big a part of the life I've lived and too much a part of who I am today.

I never saw the first ex after the divorce. I see the second regularly and consider him a friend. I wish them both well. The key to moving beyond past hurts is forgiving the other person, and even forgiving yourself. I'm often asked how I can get along so well with my ex. I wonder how can they *not?* Especially if you have children together, why on earth would you want to put yourself through that kind of bitterness? I know women who literally hate their ex-husband, the father of their children. And all it is doing is eating them up inside and hurting their children. The ex-husband really couldn't care less. So, whether you forgive and move on because it is the right thing to do or simply to preserve your sanity, just do it. Everyone wins in the long run. And now, back to our story...

Despite finding law school more difficult than I'd expected, I still thought I was living a fairy-tale life; and of course the first thing a good fairy tale needs is a checklist. (Well, maybe not; but that seemed logical to me at the time.) The first item on that fairy-tale checklist was locating a handsome prince. I hadn't come across Mr. Right in college (probably not helped by the fact that I moved around all over the place in my efforts to make sure I graduated early). But now I was the ripe old age of twenty, so it was time to start ticking the boxes of my dream life with my dream prince.

In my first year of law school, I met a young man at church who was an undergraduate student (though he was only a few months younger than me, since I was always in a hurry). He was the perfect catch: extremely handsome, athletic, and smart. He had been the quarterback of his high school football team, salutatorian of his class, and voted "Most Handsome." Well, you can see why Miss "Most Studious" over here thought she had found a real winner!

I was infatuated with his charm and natural good looks, and I think he liked the fact that I was in law school. Why wouldn't he, when that was likely to lead to a very nice period of our living as DINKs (Double Income, No Kids)? So, we got engaged. So young. Too young. Why? Partly to start living the fairy tale, but mostly to have sex.

We had both been raised with conservative, Christian values, which I still hold. But, boy, being twenty or twenty-one years old is *so* young to get married, or even to know what you want out of life. However, I can say with some certainty that had he remained interested in the marriage, I would still be married to him—because that's how I was raised, and it's who I am.

We got married in a beautiful ceremony. I planned every detail, stretching our tiny budget to doomsday because that's what I do.

I'd wanted fresh flower garlands swagged across the front of the sanctuary, but there was no budget for lavish flowers. That wasn't going to stop me! My friend and I drove around east Texas looking for wild ivy, clipping long strands of it, and throwing it in the back of my car. Then, since my home in Marshall was only an hour from Tyler, Texas—the rose capital of the world—we went to Tyler and stopped at numerous road-side stands where they sold "Tyler Roses" for a dollar a dozen. We hit every stand we could, buying all of their pink or white roses. We must have bought sixty dozen, for the bargain price of $60! Then we wired together the strands to make garlands and attached the roses and some baby's breath throughout. The result was beautiful, and I was so proud of it.

I may have had a poor Cinderella's budget, but my wedding was fit for a princess.

OUR WEDDING NIGHT AND THE START OF MY NEW LIFE

The wedding was beautiful. Everything went perfectly and according to the checklist.

Then we got into our waiting carriage—make that a limousine—which took us twelve miles down the road to a charming, historic hotel in Jefferson, Texas. What was supposed to be one of the first, glorious boxes to check—our *honeymoon*—turned out to be a nightmare.

The long-awaited, first sexual encounter simply proved far too painful to bear. Try as I might, I couldn't stand the pain. Could it be that I was failing in my first official role as princess? I still have gruesome memories of blood all over the black and white hexagon tile in the bathroom and lots and lots of tears. As bad as the physical pain was, the most unbearable part of the night was seeing his disappointment—even anger. Unsatisfied, I'm sure, in fulfilling *his own* version of the fairy tale, he ended the night by falling asleep, sullen, not speaking to me, with his back turned to me while I cried myself to sleep. Epic fairy tale fail!

I have since learned of many other young women who have had a similar experience. Some of them had husbands who were patient and loving and eased them through this phase.

Others I know had husbands who acted much like mine, and they ended their marriage almost immediately. Hopefully, this is a sign that today's enlightened woman knows her worth and refuses to accept this kind of treatment.

The truth is that the handwriting was on the wall that very first night. A man who reacts that way to not having his needs met probably just doesn't love you enough to go the distance in life. Had he loved me enough, he would naturally have been disappointed that his own fairy-tale desires weren't met that night, but he would never have left me to cry myself to sleep.

As tends to happen with newlyweds, however, we got everything sorted out in the bedroom with a little practice and carried on with our new married life.

Everything went splendidly at first. He was studying accounting, which is a tough major—and, as it turns out, one that wasn't in his wheelhouse. So, he switched his major. Well, he tried, anyway. Apparently, the new major was an even *more* competitive program to enter.

I graduated law school two months after turning twenty-three and was hired by a firm in north Texas. I was thankful to have a job! After we moved, my husband still had work to do on his undergraduate degree, but he was able to transfer to a university nearby where he was finally able to switch to a new major.

I spent the summer after graduation studying for the bar. What an experience! You wouldn't think that after spending three years in law school you would *still* need a six-week course, six days per week, to prepare to pass the bar, the license that would allow you to actually practice. But you do! Then you take the test—two-and-a-half *days* of testing! Even worse, you *then* wait six more weeks for your results. (At least, that's how it worked in 1990.)

In the meantime, I started working for my new law firm with the understanding that if I failed, they may or may not fire me.

Once I finally knew that I had passed the bar, life was underway. I had officially ticked some major boxes on my checklist—all by the age of twenty-three!

EVEN SLIGHTLY SQUARE PEGS DON'T FIT IN ROUND HOLES

One of the lessons that took me the longest to learn was that the way you plan your life is almost certainly not how your life will turn out. That doesn't mean it can't be far *better* than you imagined. It just means it will rarely be the exact *way* you imagined it. But since my life was destined to be a fairy tale, I naturally assumed I could map it out from the beginning, much the way I mapped out my college curriculum.

What I hadn't learned yet, but soon would, was that I had to get away from my tendency to think I could make anything work. In my youth, I still thought I could figure anything out—that I could take a slightly square peg and put it in a slightly round hole, because it didn't really matter. I checked off enough boxes in my life checklist that I knew this was just *going to work*. I was going to will it to be so.

Even as I started to see signs that perhaps things were not working out as planned in this marriage, I still thought I could work harder, do something *more*, and I'd get it all back under control.

At that age, we still believe in what we're told about how life is supposed to work. So, when things don't go as planned, it feels like we've failed. But whatever people are telling you about how life is supposed to work is baloney, because *they don't know*. None of us knows. Everything is about choosing which should be the next door to open, and we simply cannot see those doors at only twenty years old, or twenty-three, or even throughout our twenties or early thirties sometimes.

We put so much pressure on kids to know something they aren't equipped yet to discover. I mean, we graduate from high school at seventeen or eighteen years old, and then college at twenty, twenty-one, or twenty-two, and we're told, "You're an adult now. Go out in the world and determine how the rest of your life is going to shake out."

At the same time, we tell kids, "This is how your life is sup- posed to look," despite knowing there's not just *one way* a life is supposed to look—especially now, with so many opportunities available to us, and so many ways of working and living. But we're still telling them the same things, at least by implication.

I've been in the strange position now, as an adult, where people in their twenties sometimes ask me, "How do you know what to do?"

Recently, a kid who was still in high school wanted to have breakfast with me, to talk about his options. I met with him, and he said, "I want to go to law school—maybe Baylor or UT

Law School when I'm finished with college. What books should I be reading?"

I didn't know what to tell him! He has so much time to figure all that out. And besides, there's no magic list of books I can give you that will guarantee success in the future!

Ultimately, I told him, "If you want to read books, that's great. But, more importantly, just do whatever job is at hand to the very best of your ability—and don't spend so much of your time worrying about stuff you can't yet control. Do your best, but also have a good time along the way!"

Any one of us could get hit by a bus tomorrow. Do you really want to spend your last day worried about something so far down the road that you don't enjoy the time you have *now*? Again, whatever you think right now that you're going to do for the rest of your life, I promise you it won't be that. I don't know what it's going to be, but I do know it's not going to be what you plan when you're in high school, or even in college and beyond, because that is incredibly rare.

Still, what you end up doing might be a million times better than what you're currently planning! So, quit worrying so much about that end point, which is nearly impossible to know. Just focus on the next step while finding joy in every day. That's the balance. That's the whole ticket.

I had to go through the complete dissolution of every item on my checklist before I learned this lesson. Maybe now you can learn it from me, so you won't have to learn the hard way as much as I did!

A SINKING FEELING

My job at the law firm paid most of the bills while my husband was still trying to finish school and working part time at a local nonprofit, assisting the director in marketing and public relations. It was a good fit for him. In fact, he seemed to enjoy it more and more, staying at work longer and longer. His boss—a woman around fifteen years older than he was—started becoming the center of most of his stories about work each day.

From the day he started work, I was told later, she moved his desk into her office. Ah, the perils of marrying a handsome man. Honestly, he—and we—probably never stood a chance once this older woman took an interest in him. Flattery and attention is a powerful drug for most people—and, I believe, especially for men.

At a festival the museum was hosting, she actually sat in his lap and asked him, in baby talk voice, if he had been talking to "that woman." Then I realized she meant me! The person I am today would have handled the situation differently (for better or worse), but I just stood there, stunned that he was sitting right in front of me, allowing her to speak this way. And yet I still couldn't accept that anything could *really* be going on between them. Where on earth is *that* in any fairy tale you've ever read?

One morning, she showed up at our house around five to pick him up so they could appear on a local radio morning show, to talk about an upcoming fundraising event. I didn't like that at all, but what could I do? He ignored me every time I even brought up her name.

I tuned in to the radio show and was horrified to hear the DJ joke that the two of them were "fighting like an old married couple." He was right. Their banter was very natural. They sounded like we had in our early days, joking and teasing one another, and clearly having a great time. I was beginning to develop a real sense of unease about everything, including our entire future together.

Things got weirder from there. He started having nightmares and acting out in his sleep. I once woke up with him on top of me, holding me by my wrists and screaming, "Give me that videotape!" He pushed me out of the bed and against the wall. I am just grateful to this day that he woke up before going any farther!

Since he was having this "issue," he slept for a while in the guest room. I told my best friend from high school I was worried about his sleeping alone where I couldn't watch him. I asked, "What if he somehow hurts himself or sticks his head in the toilet and drowns?"

I still remember her answer: "Better him than you!"

He and his boss began traveling for work, and while on the road he would buy little gifts for this woman's child. Again, I didn't like that one bit. I told him that was a huge source of flattery for a woman—paying attention to her child—and that his boss could take it the wrong way. For that matter, so could her husband! Of course, it all fell on deaf ears. Or worse, maybe I was giving him a roadmap for how to win her affection—as if he needed any help!

As you have probably already figured out, it soon became obvious that they were *already* in a relationship.

All I could think was, *Things like this don't happen to people like me*. Or people like him! We were good kids, who had met at church, and planned to be married for life.

Shortly after that trip, he told me he was going to stay on a friend's couch for a while to "figure things out." What on earth was there to figure out? In my mind, we were fine. We weren't fighting. Life was excruciatingly normal! Nevertheless, he moved out with hardly an explanation. He wouldn't tell me where he was going or even *why*.

I'll never forget my wonderfully wise mother telling me I could count on his being with another woman. She said, "A man doesn't leave the nest unless he's got another nest to go to."

We talked about going to counseling with a counselor provided by our church. He stood me up time and time again, so I went by myself. The counselor gave me priceless advice. I said, "I know he would like for me to cook more or spend more time on the house." You have to understand, I was grabbing at straws here, as this whole situation had completely blindsided me. She told me that nothing in this situation was about me, and that people who are looking to leave will antagonize their partner, hoping to get a response from them so they can say, "See how you are?" She assured me that no amount of cooking, cleaning, or anything else could fix what was going on here.

That counselor also told me something I never forgot: that I wasn't really grieving the relationship with *him*, since it could not have been *that* fulfilling, but I was instead grieving the death of the dream. Being a conservative Christian girl, I had always dreamed—make that *assumed*—I would have a picket fence with rocking chairs on the porch and spend my life with the one and only man I had married. Having this marriage end after only three and a half years was devastating. Was I really going to be a divorced person? That was not in my plan at all!

That was when I first started learning that life has a way of teaching you that you aren't nearly as in control as you think you are. "The best laid plans of mice and men." There's nothing wrong with planning. In fact, there is something very wrong with a failure to plan. But, in our planning, we need to remember that we are developing a rough road map, and there *will* be twists and turns we can't foresee. There will be detours, some of them glorious and some of them extremely painful.

SINK OR SWIM?

Of course, I wasn't the kind of person who could "let it go" and just move on from my *husband* moving on from me. He was telling me virtually nothing, but I still needed to understand. I didn't even know how to find him or reach him! This was 1992, and no one had cell phones. So I waited for him to call.

I even asked my mom, "How can I find out where he lives or what he's doing?"

She said, "You wake up real early on Sunday morning when everyone is home and in bed, and you drive through every apartment parking lot until you find his car. He *will* be home at that time of day."

I did. I drove through a few nearby apartment complexes and, lo and behold, she was right. My mother usually was.

It didn't take me long to find his car. But now what? I didn't know which apartment he was actually *in*. So I went back later and did something I can still hardly believe I did. You can grow a shocking amount of nerve and boldness when you are *mad* that your life, your plan, and all your dreams are being derailed by someone making what you believe to be very stupid choices! I walked into the apartment office and lied. Something I *just don't do*. But I did, and I learned right then that you can be so angry you just don't care. I told the young girl working there I had come to see my friend but had lost the number of his apartment. I guess I looked convincing and innocent enough. She pulled out her file and gave me the number I needed!

Off to his apartment I marched. I banged and banged and banged on the door, calling out for him to open up. He wouldn't let me in, but I could hear him on the other side of the door saying he would call me later. I could hear whispering and shuffling too; she must have been with him. I may not have been able to force his hand completely, but it still gave me a little satisfaction knowing that *he* knew I had busted him. Not much of a victory, but when your world is falling apart, you'll find comfort in the smallest of things.

I continued going to counseling, and he continued failing to show up. So, before long, the die was cast. It was time to move forward with filing for divorce. I needed to begin to accept that my life was not going to be the life I thought I would lead.

And I had no idea how to start rescripting my life.

My mother, as usual, gave me the best advice, saying, "He's

thought long and hard about this, you can bet. And he's not coming back."

She did not set me up for failure by encouraging me to fight for something that was gone. But, being me, I fought until it was obvious it was over.

I did not want to be a divorced person, and none of this was *my* idea or in my plan, so I wasn't about to be the one to file the divorce papers. Since I was an attorney, he obviously wanted me to do the paperwork and filing so it would be "free." The solution I came up with was to draft the papers in his name and send them over to him along with instructions on where to take them and how to pay the fee. I wasn't about to let him perpetrate a lie that I had filed for divorce. This was *all his choice*, and I wanted that on public record.

We were young and didn't have much yet, but we had bought a new little home—my very first real estate purchase. Thank goodness we didn't have any children. We simply split up the credit card bills we had, and I kept the house, since I was the only one with enough income at the time to make the payments.

Shortly after the divorce, I listed the house for sale and sold it quickly for a nice profit, which paid off *all* the bills I had taken out of the marriage! This was the first—but would not be the last—time that real estate came to my rescue! He saw what I sold the house for and of course contacted me to see if I was going to share the profit with him. Um, no! Had real estate prices dropped, I would have been the one assuming all the risk. So, at least financially, I was the one who came out, as my mom would say, "smelling like a rose!"

Thanks to the divorce, 1992 was one of the hardest years of my life. My ex never admitted the affair to me. Being a conservative Christian, I would have felt more comfortable in my right to remarry with confirmation that he had committed adultery—which he knew very well, being from the same upbringing. So, I had a phone call with him once toward the end, asking him to at least give me that, to state the obvious truth. But he acted so weird and would *only* repeat the following robotic phrase (that I can only assume she gave him to say to me): "I have found love and happiness, and so can you."

He said that over and over, no matter how many times I asked the question. Like someone pleading the Fifth! That brought out the lawyer in me, and I cross-examined him, saying, "We clearly have different opinions on what is allowable in life, so I am only asking for the facts rather than whether *you* think I can 'find love and happiness.'" Oh, the exhaustion of it all.

Looking back, we just married too young. In hindsight, I probably wrangled him right into my checklist plan of marriage long before he was ready for that kind of commitment. I never saw him again, and we simply went our separate ways. Since we never had children, it honestly feels more like he was someone I dated for a while and things just didn't work out. I rarely think of him; but from what I can see from a quick internet search, he has been successful in his career and seems to have a happy life. I'm glad. Holding onto resentments is never a prescription for happiness. It's a prescription for an ulcer, high blood pressure, and alienation of those closest to us—nothing I want to have any part of.

BECOMING STRONGER BY CHOOSING TO BE HAPPY

Of course, I look back at that situation *now* and wish him the best. At the time, not so much.

The stress of that time took me down to ninety-eight pounds. Not on purpose—I simply had no appetite. Some people eat when they're really stressed; I lose my appetite.

I had lived this life where I was always excelling, getting ahead, doing the right thing, never getting in trouble, literally being the perfect kid, and thinking, *Well, I've done everything just so, and my love's going to be perfect, because I followed all the rules.* Needless to say, my first restart was both unexpected and deeply jarring.

Although you are going to read about later restarts I had to go through, this first restart was, without a doubt, the hardest. Others may have affected me far greater in the long term, but my first divorce had such a jarring impact when it happened because it was so unexpected.

That first restart was the one that was *never going to* happen. There was no way I was going to be married for three and a half years and then get divorced. I didn't believe in divorce. He didn't believe in divorce. It was just not ever a possibility.

This restart shook me far more than the second one; by then, I had enough life experience to know that things aren't always as they seem, and life's not perfect. Learning that first hard lesson, though, was much more difficult.

When you're really young, you think you can *will* things to be...

well, if not perfect, then at least good. And it's surprising the first time you learn that you can't do that. Everything I'd ever wanted to control the outcome of, I'd been able to—until then. Suddenly, that myth was over at age twenty-four, and I could never go back to that innocence again.

When that life path—go to school, go to college, get a job, get married, have kids—evaporates for the first time, you just don't know where to go anymore.

You may be in your twenties, or you may have people in your life who are in their twenties; and that first restart is coming—if it hasn't hit already. It may not be a divorce; it could be going to school to study in a certain major and then realizing you can't pass the courses. It could be starting a new job and realizing that the career you've worked so hard for isn't actually one that fulfills you. A lot of people at that age are going through major life changes. When it's your first time experiencing that sudden restart, it can be painful and hard to get your head around.

All my friends were incredibly supportive during this time. And, of course, over the next months, I grew stronger. I realized, to my amazement, that the world had not ended. That's when mom would remind me about the despair I had been in. She would say, "And now things are better; so let's remember next time when something goes wrong, those days don't last forever. So we only let ourselves go so far down."

My mom was a mindset warrior before the word mindset became part of mainstream culture. She wanted me to stop and analyze how miserable I had allowed myself to feel when just a few short weeks later life was looking up again. Her point was to learn that the pain can be very real, but still not be the end of the world. Every hurt thereafter, I put into a little more perspective. And it hurt a little bit less because I *knew* I could survive anything that came my way.

This is one of the best lessons I can share with you. Hard times of all shapes and sizes will come for all of us, I'm afraid. Life has taught me the best thing we can do in the moment is harness all of our willpower to remind ourselves that better times *will* come. The sun *will* shine again.

I believe happiness is a product of what we choose to think about. The Bible even says this in Philippians 4:8, "...whatever is true, whatever is noble, whatever is right, whatever is pure, whatever is lovely, whatever is admirable—if anything is excellent or praiseworthy—think about such things."

I have had friends and coworkers ask me, "Doesn't anything make you upset?" Well, of course I get upset! But I believe, through years of training my mind to be strong, I'm able to *choose* what to think about. There have been many times when situations were tough at work, in my business, when any *normal* person would have tossed and turned all night worrying about what to do. I've had great success using a technique where I force myself to flip a mental switch and think about something pleasant. I tell myself I can only do two useful things: I can either get up and do something productive to solve the issue at hand, or I can get some sleep so I will have the energy in the morning to tackle the problem with a fresh mindset. I'm simply too determined to live a happy life, with few regrets, to allow being upset to bring me down for one moment longer than necessary.

How do you do that? You just think some thought that makes you happy and relaxed. Maybe picture a beautiful trip you want to take some day. Maybe think of a fun memory you have made in the past. Today, we even have tools and shortcuts we can use, such as apps that help put us into a relaxing, calm state. Worrying and exhausting yourself is not going to make solving the problem tomorrow any easier.

When I went through this first divorce, the loss of my perfect little future was extremely painful. Every morning when I first woke up, I was once again slapped in the face with the fact that my husband was gone, and I would soon be a divorced woman. That was very difficult for me to accept. But I had to get out of bed. I had to work. Life was going to plod on whether I felt up to it or not. So, here's what I did that can work for you as well: I chose my positive, affirming mantra. For me it was two hymns, and I sang them. I sang them in the shower. I sang them loudly and with conviction. I sang them like I meant them. Even though the words of comfort and positivity did not feel real in those early days, I believed them in my brain. And I knew I could force my heart to accept them if I was persistent. So, I sang them each and every morning—sometimes, more than once.

The first song (based on a Bible verse) was a simple one that my high school math teacher would sing or quote every morning at the beginning of class. "This is the day that the Lord has made. I will rejoice and be glad in it" (Psalm 118:24). I didn't just sing it. I focused intently on each word, changing up which one I emphasized as I sang. For example, one time it was *this* is the day the Lord has made. I *will* rejoice and be glad in it." I was willing my heart to listen to my mind. There was no room for wallowing or self-pity in this song. Those emotions would not be my companions!

I would then sing the other: "Teach me Lord to wait down upon my knees, 'til in your own good time, you will answer my pleas. Teach me not to rely on what others say or do, but to wait in prayer for an answer from you. Those who wait upon the Lord shall renew their strength; they shall mount up with wings like eagles. They shall run and not grow weary; they shall walk and not faint. Teach me Lord, teach me Lord...to wait."

I was training my heart to wait. To walk through pain. Not to avoid, but to wait. I knew our God was mighty enough to save and mighty enough to bring me through the worst pain and embarrassment of my young life. I sang it like I meant it, and day by day it got just a little easier. When I have hard times, I still go back to those songs. They have always been a comfort and a strength to me.

And although I didn't know it at the time, after that first restart, I would need all the strength I had—because things were about to change completely and irrevocably.

CHAPTER 4

═══

BLOWING EVERYTHING UP

I will be the first to admit that I did not love practicing law. But I *did* love being in court. Unfortunately, there is shockingly little of that in the early years of practicing. There are many, many lonely quiet hours in the library, researching and writing papers.

I began my law practice right on the cusp of the days when computers were becoming commonplace. Don't get me wrong; this was the 1990s, and all the secretaries and legal assistants were clicking away on their keyboards. But we attorneys were expected to use old-school Dictaphones to dictate our work aloud into a little microphone. I had been using a word processor all through school, so verbally creating a fifty-page brief was a new and uncomfortable skill to learn! The theory was, we were paid—or should I say, the firm billed clients—$100 or more per hour for our time, so we shouldn't "waste" our time typing. I was much more efficient at typing and correcting myself. But instead, we dictated our letters and briefs, our secretaries put them in our in-boxes, and we took our red pens and made corrections. Many corrections. Many times. Oh, the number of trees we must have killed.

Also, like many attorneys, I'm afraid, I hated the first few weeks of practicing law. I wondered, *How am I going to do this for the rest of my life?* I think part of the mental toughness training they put you through is brutal but necessary.

I was assigned a research project where I spent a few days in the library digging into a complicated legal issue. This was back before the days of Google searches, so we had to research by referencing and cross-referencing law books. I honestly can't believe we found anything even remotely accurate. And worse, we were never sure we had found everything that was important. Had we missed one case tucked away in one book?

I did my research, wrote my brief, and felt pretty good about it. Then the partner who assigned the project popped his head into my office and said, "Is this right?" I assured him that I felt confident I had come to the right conclusion. I'll never forget his response: "I hope so, because there's half a million dollars riding on it."

That's a lot of pressure!

I was definitely feeling more like the pre-princess Cinderella once again. We were expected to work from eight in the morning until six in the evening during the week and spend a minimum of half a day on Saturday at the office—but the more, the better. Honestly, that schedule was never even enough to bill the expected 1,900-plus hours per year. Just being at work didn't count; we also had to write down our time in fifteen-minute increments. Knowing it would be billed directly to clients, we had to be 100 percent focused during that time. It may not have been impossible, but it sure was challenging.

Having always excelled at whatever I did, this new world felt strange and, frankly, awful. Whatever I did, I never felt like it was enough. And what was worse, I looked at the senior partners—those who had "made it" in our office—and they were at the office *far* longer than I was and didn't seem any happier than I was.

To stay really motivated, I think people need to see "an end in sight." Not an end to working, since the Bible says that "if a man doesn't work, neither shall he eat," but an end to being owned by the clock. Do you have an "end in sight?" And I don't mean complete retirement, because—for me, at least—that is the very definition of waiting to die! I mean a time when the workload will change in a way that is meaningful to you. If you aren't happy doing what you are doing currently and have no actionable plan or vision of it changing, career satisfaction (and, probably, overall happiness) will continue to elude you.

There was certainly no end in sight for me. I wondered how I would ever have a family, attend dance recitals, and take my kids to birthday parties if working all week plus much of the weekend was really considered a *minimum* standard.

But, what could I do? I had this law degree, and I had bills to pay.

EVERYTHING CHANGES

I kept working, and life moved on after my divorce.

I had my own apartment. I had a new car, a Mitsubishi 3000 GT. It was black and loud and fast—and awesome! I was enjoying my job a little more; I had found a lane, and life in general was becoming more full and more enjoyable. I joined the Junior League, a women's charity organization, giving me another thing to occupy my time and my focus. The world was starting to feel like my oyster once again.

However, the little town where I lived in north Texas was *not* the best place to be single. It is a *great* family town, but the singles scene is slim pickings!

There were some guys, some dates. I recall after one of those dates, another attorney in our firm asked how it went, and I told her it was fine. She asked if I was going to see him again. "Not on purpose," I answered as I just kept walking down the hall.

I did have one serious relationship with a private pilot who had been a Navy pilot, *Top Gun* style. I was crazy about him, but our backgrounds and future goals were different. So, in 1994, we agreed to go our separate ways as things didn't seem to be working out.

On the night of October 20, 1994, however, everything changed.

That night, I attended the weekly Junior League meeting and came home around nine, pulling up to the new-to-me house I lived in and had been fixing up. (This was the second house I had bought since the divorce. I think the real estate bug was kicking in!) I went inside and got ready for bed with my cat, Toonces—yes, the driving cat if you're an *SNL* fan.

About an hour later, right as I was falling asleep, I was rocked by a loud explosion in my house. I immediately reached into my bedside drawer and took out the small pistol I kept there (this was Texas, after all!). I could not figure out what had happened, but I knew it couldn't be good. I could hear glass from the windows in the other rooms continuing to crash onto the floor. I was sure an intruder was in my house. So, I did what you're supposed to do and dialed 911.

They listened to my situation, and—I'll never forget—the dispatcher said, "It's probably your hot water heater; we'll send someone over."

Then she hung up. Well, that didn't seem right! I watched a lot of the TV shows like *Rescue 911* with William Shatner back in those days, and if I knew one thing, it was that the operator was supposed to keep you on the line!

So, I decided to call my parents while I waited...in the dark... hearing sounds in the other room...with my door cracked and my little pistol cocked and aimed at the opening. Both parents were on separate phones. I whispered to my mom that someone was in my house. In hindsight, being a mom now myself, I probably shouldn't have done this; I can't imagine being ten hours from my child and having them tell me there was an intruder in their home! How helpless and panicked she must have felt. My dad was terrified, too, I'm sure, but he kept saying, "What?" and "Huh?" Typical man, right? Then I heard my mom on the other line saying, "James, be quiet!"

I whispered as loudly as I could, "I really can't speak up at the moment, since there's a robber in my house!"

I knew my folks were desperate for any information as they waited silently on the other line, hearts beating loudly in their ears, so I assured them, "My gun is cocked, I've said my prayers, and I'm taking him with me!" And in that moment, I had no doubt that I 100 percent *would* shoot him to defend myself.

What felt like an hour later—but was probably really only about five minutes—the other line beeped (I was high-tech at the time and had call waiting!). I clicked over, and it was 911 calling *me* back, thank you very much! She let me know the officer was outside and told me to go answer the door. I was understandably hesitant, as I had continued hearing glass shatter and crunch in the living room outside my door. She assured me he had checked the windows and that no one was inside the house. So, in the dark, I slowly, quietly made my way to the front door, looking around for the intruder I had been hearing. My heart was pounding so hard, but I just knew if I could make it to the front door where the police officer was, then everything would be all right.

I slowly opened the front door to what I thought was a rainstorm. Water was falling everywhere as the officer greeted me. I was so confused that I asked, "Is it raining?"

"No, but you have a broken water line... Something exploded."

I told him I could hear someone walking around inside, and he pointed out that all the windows across the front of my house were shattered and the glass was simply continuing to fall. That was the sound I had been hearing.

THE PLOT THICKENS

Over the next few hours, life got really interesting. I called an attorney friend from work, who lived a few blocks away, since the police said I would need to stay somewhere else for a while. She came over immediately and said she and her husband heard the explosion. By this time, the police were putting yellow tape around my yard and telling me that my water heater had not exploded—but that a *bomb* had been placed in my mailbox and had detonated.

The house I lived in was built in the 1950s, and it had one of those mailboxes built into the side of the house. When the postman would put mail into the slot, the mail would fall onto the living room floor. Remember those? Well, believe it or not, someone had actually stuck a homemade bomb into that slot. Luckily, it was too large to fall through. I had not checked my mail that evening when I returned home late from Junior League—thank goodness! The officer said if I had stuck my hand in there, it would have been blown off.

My friend and I sat at the kitchen table and did what lawyers do: I pulled out my homeowner policy, and we started reviewing my coverage. I was relieved to see that acts of vandalism or criminal acts were covered. I could easily see that there was a hole in the soffit on my front porch, and there were at least six windows were broken out across the front part of the house.

I stepped outside and had the thought run through my mind, *Boy, some helpful neighbors I have! No one is even stepping outside to check on me. I know it's late, but that explosion was pretty loud!* I later found out that numerous men in the neighborhood had run out into the street carrying shotguns and rifles and were all ordered by the police to get back inside their houses. At a moving sale I had a few weeks later, one neighbor who lived eight houses away told me he had gotten home late and was eating soup when the explosion shook the bowl in his hand.

I spent the night with my friend, packing up Toonces and taking him with me in his cat carrier. It takes a special friend to welcome you into their home in the middle of the night after someone has apparently just tried to kill you. I will say, she did ask me to park my car a bit down the street, not directly in front of her house!

The next day, my mom made the ten-hour drive up from East Texas. Here I was once again, Miss Fairy Tale Princess, somehow getting into trouble! Together, we rented a hotel room under a different name. There is something very eerie about not knowing who has just tried to harm you and why.

Officers from the Bureau of Alcohol, Tobacco, Firearms and Explosives, or ATF, appeared at my office the next day and asked to speak to me. It's never good when you're just a regular gal, minding your own business, and the ATF needs to speak to you! I told them, "I pretty much go to work, to church, and to Junior League meetings. How does any of this make sense?"

Everyone jumped to the conclusion that it was related to my work. I told them, "I don't practice *that* kind of law; nothing I do gets anyone excited enough to put a bomb in my house!"

Everyone's next thought was that it was my ex-boyfriend, the pilot, but that never made sense to me. Our breakup was very mutual. We got along well, but I was probably more ready to settle down than he was; plus, we had religious differences. Again, there was no animosity—and no reason at all to bomb me, for goodness' sake!

But I remembered that I had been receiving some strange, harassing phone calls in the past few weeks...even while he and I were still together. In fact, he was far more concerned about the calls than I was. For a while, people—mostly men—had been calling me asking about the AR-15 Sporter rifle I had listed in the *Thrifty Nickel* newspaper. Then they started asking about the 1973 Corvette car body I had for sale at a super cheap price. Of course, I had never listed any such thing in the *Thrifty Nickel*. My boyfriend had been very concerned and gone down to the publication's office. They said the ads were paid for in cash by a white male with dark hair, as best they could recall. Apparently, both items were listed far below market value, with the intention that people would call relentlessly about them, thereby harassing me. Boy, those were simpler times, when that was someone's idea of a way to harass another person!

After a few days in the hotel under the pseudonym, I found a furnished apartment with security, the only such building in town. It wasn't cheap, but I just couldn't stay by myself after this without some sense of extra safety. The ATF officers had told me they were particularly concerned because the device in my mailbox had both a timer and touch trigger. They said it was much more sophisticated than a typical pipe bomb they would expect to see if area delinquents had made it and randomly placed it in my mailbox. It was designed to go off when I checked the mail—or, if I didn't check the mail, it would go off at a certain time, when I would be in bed, probably twenty feet away from where it was placed. The officers said I should take the matter seriously, and they needed to show me how to check under the hood of my car and underneath the frame before starting my car each time.

That's when I knew it was time to move!

MY MAIN SUSPECT

I told the police about *my* prime suspect. There was a young man in our young, married couples group at church who seemed overly interested in me, considering the fact that he was married. He called me at work once and said, "Hey, I heard you've been speeding around in that sports car of yours!" I was obviously concerned that this strange guy I barely knew was apparently spying on me *and* felt it necessary to call me at work to say so. He finally admitted he heard on his police scanner that I had been pulled over for speeding (on the way to an after-church party, lest you think I was doing something really exciting). I told him I didn't have time for this conversation and hung up, very creeped out.

My mom had visited town just a couple weeks before the bomb and had attended church with me. She remembered attending a special breakfast hosted there where she saw this same guy across from me in line trying to make conversation. She said I gave him one of my "go to h-e-double-l" looks. I told her he was behaving inappropriately, calling me at work and making flirty comments with his poor wife standing right there.

The police went to his house to question him and agreed it was odd that when they asked where he was, his wife said she wasn't sure and didn't question them. If your husband is normal, you show alarm when police are at the door looking for him! Apparently he had an alibi of some sort for the time frame they believe the bomb was placed. But let's face it: he could have had someone else place the bomb in my mailbox, and I believe he did. Why do I think it was him? Because of his hobbies. Our church class sent out a questionnaire to everyone so we could all get to know each other better. It asked for basic info in addition to our hobbies. His background was military; he reported that his hobbies were shooting and collecting guns, and classic car restoration. What are the odds? Those correlate with the two "for sale" items placed in the *Thrifty Nickel*.

For whatever reason, the authorities couldn't or didn't go any further with it, and I simply wasn't willing to live life every day checking under the hood of my car. During this time period, I developed a real empathy for those with Post Traumatic Stress Disorder (PTSD), and I suffered from it for many months after the explosion. The interesting thing about PTSD is that you actually relive the trauma, rather than just thinking about it or remembering it. You dream about it, but it feels as real as the day it happened. You wake up in a sweat, with your heart racing, exactly as if you just experienced it again.

The security apartment I rented was in a very tall building, and I was on an upper floor. I remember needing to go from the kitchen to the bedroom, but there were windows all around the room. So I would literally crawl on my hands and knees to my bedroom so that whoever could be out there watching me through binoculars...or a scope...couldn't see me. It was a horrible time, and I knew it was my time to leave town. I just had to hope that whoever had tried to hurt or kill me wouldn't follow.

SOMETIMES, THE BRAVEST THING TO DO IS MAKE A CHANGE

Sometimes, life is going to put you where you need to be—and some of the ways it gets you there are going to be unpleasant and completely unforeseen.

I had no intention of leaving town, but apparently that was meant to be (and would ultimately lead to marrying my second husband, having kids, and starting our business together; but I'm getting ahead of myself).

Crazy stuff is going to happen along the way. How are you going to react to that? It's going to be hard at the time, and you're not immediately going to be a mindset hero and just bounce through it. But maybe if you know these things can happen, they will be less surprising when they come.

Later, once you have moved past it, you can look back and recognize that crazy stuff happens, and it can still be okay. When I'm in those moments, when something's bad, I take comfort in remembering times in my life, or in someone else's, where this happened and we're okay. The most comforting thing to me when I went through that first divorce was being told by someone whose name I've forgotten but whose story stays with me, "I've been through it. You won't believe me today, but you're going to be okay. You're going to be happy. This is all going to be in the rearview mirror."

When bad things happen to you, you can remember, "Well, shoot, Tammy had a bomb in her house. That's pretty bad, but she's okay. Maybe I can keep going, too."

You can't give up; you have to just keep going. When you're going through it, when it feels really immediate, you might think, *I'm never going to be happy again*, or *I'm never going to feel safe again*. But you will. It just takes time. Eventually, you are going to be happy. Whatever happened to you is going to be in the rearview mirror, and you're gonna learn something from it.

If you choose to share your story, maybe somebody else can learn something from it, too—even if the biggest takeaway is that you got through and you're okay, so that other people can know they'll be able to do the same.

In that moment, this experience was the most important thing ever. I never would've imagined a day would go by when it wouldn't be on my mind. But now, it's a story I tell at cocktail parties or a fun fact to use in "Three Truths and a Lie."

Some of your most devastating happenings may end up just being interesting anecdotes one day. They're absolutely not going to feel like the same heaviness that they feel today.

Knowing that doesn't cure it today, but it gives you hope. Often, we can make it to the next day, as long as we have hope that tomorrow it'll hurt even 1 percent less. And the day after that, 1 percent less. We just need hope to get to tomorrow knowing what we feel right now doesn't have to be what we're going to feel then, next month, or next year.

I can tell you that someday it'll be just something you'll look back on in amazement that it even happened to you.

That's exactly how it happened for me—*after* I got myself out of the situation.

MAKING MY MOVE

I had always thought I might end up in the Dallas area someday, so I started checking the DFW classified ads for attorneys.

Can you imagine how those interviews went? I ended up working for a law firm there, and when the senior partner asked why I was moving to Dallas, I told him about the bomb. He just looked at me and said, "No, really. Why are you leaving your current firm?"

Of course, he called my old firm and confirmed everything I had told him. I got the position and was able to take a few weeks off between firms—something you *never* get to do when practicing law unless you're between positions. Looking back, I realized in the four years I had practiced law I had never taken more than four days off in a row...with two of those days being the weekend!

So, I said goodbye to my friends and coworkers and loaded up the truck to head to Dallas. I found an apartment building that had twenty-four-hour security with a manned entry gate. Slowly, over the next few months, I began to relax a bit and have a little confidence that the nut who ran me out of town wasn't following me. But even that took time. As with most hard times in life, the only way to get past the bad is simply to walk through it. No shortcuts allowed, I'm afraid.

Dallas was a huge change and a very welcomed one, being that

I was single. Maybe the bomb just accelerated the move I was destined to make at some point. I visited a few local churches to find one with an active, vibrant, young singles community.

It didn't take long for me to meet someone.

Time to fire up that checklist again, I thought.

CHAPTER 5

===

RESTART #2: A NEW HUSBAND—AND A NEW CAREER

They say that hope springs eternal, and I began the new chapter of my life full of optimism that I could just treat the last several years of my life as one big dry-erase checklist. I would erase all the checkmarks and start over, basically with the exact same boxes on my list. Surely my downfall hadn't been the checklist itself, but in my execution of it, right?

I met my second husband within weeks of moving to Dallas. He was the unofficial leader of our singles group at church, very friendly, tall, dark, and authoritative. He had recently finished serving four years in the Marine Corps and had just attained the rank of captain, remaining in the Reserve. He had then gone back to school to get a degree from the University of North Texas in jazz piano. He was very serious about his music and had tremendous talent. He was diligent in class attendance and had a 4.0 GPA. This all sounded great to me! He also came from a wonderful, church-going family.

I liked being married. I preferred it, in fact. The single life really wasn't for me, and when I met him, I was already twenty-seven—almost twenty-eight—which seemed like the perfect age to settle down and start thinking about a family. He was thirty and had never been married. Neither of us had kids to complicate our lives. This seemed like the ideal situation for both of us.

Within just a few months of meeting, we were engaged. People often tell me, "Oh, you should have waited longer, and then you would have known you probably weren't really right for each other."

Maybe. But I have a theory, too: we *all* show the person we are dating who we *want* to show them. And we can all keep that front up for a good, long while. Not until the ink is dry do we really let our guard down.

Besides, what could go wrong? He was back in school but had some benefits from being in the Reserve and could work making captain's pay during school holidays. I had a good job as an attorney. We had a lot of background in common. In fact, we had both been students at Abilene Christian at the same time, but we had never met each other. He always said that's because he was on the five-year plan, and I was on the three-year plan. I'm sure he had more fun, but, then again, I had fun getting ahead of everyone!

We had a charming wedding in a Victorian home in a small town about an hour from Dallas. Thirty or so guests watched me walk down the stairs in my short, white wedding dress—what do you wear when you have been married before but you still want the day to be special? After all, *this* was going to be the father of my children! There he stood in front of the parlor fireplace, tall and handsome, in his Marines dress blues.

After the ceremony and the reception dinner—we have short weddings in the Church of Christ since there is typically no drinking or dancing—it was time to drive away to our new life. We waved goodbye in my black sports car and drove into the night.

Although this wedding night was certainly better than before, I almost thought I perceived a very slight lessening of interest in me from the start. The passion we had felt during our courtship seemed to have cooled just ever so slightly. Was the chasing of me more fun than the catching? He certainly wouldn't be the first person to feel that way, I'm sure.

I banished the thought and said grace that I wasn't going through what I had the first time around.

ANOTHER LESS-THAN-STELLAR HONEYMOON

For our honeymoon, we went to his family's cabin in the mountains. The views were beautiful, and the price was right for our newlywed budget, but I continued to feel him distancing himself from me. This made no sense to me. We hadn't had a disagreement. What on earth was going on *this* time?

After I questioned him on it several times, he finally told me what was on his mind.

He had told me when we met that he had been a bit of a rounder or partier in the past. That didn't really bother me, as I expected that most men had gone through a phase of sowing their wild oats. What did bother me was that he had not only been involved in partying early in his life but had also continued to do so as recently as his bachelor party, just a few days before—and, more importantly, it had all been done behind my back.

Now, understand that the things he was confessing to me would probably be considered *very* minor to you, and probably even to me at my age now. But at that time, I was the queen of Goody Two-shoes and had zero tolerance for anything more than absolute tee-totaling abstinence. Having no flexibility at that stage of my life, I was devastated. We are a product of our experiences, so I'm sure my reaction was greatly influenced by having my first marriage not work out. Could it be possible that I was on high alert?

Now that the ink had dried on the marriage certificate, he thought this would be a good time to unburden himself. On our honeymoon. Can you imagine the sinking feeling I had—*again*?

Looking back, my feelings may have been a bit extreme, but they felt very real and very normal at the time. If these were small things, why not tell me about them *before* we married rather than on our honeymoon? Another disappointing honeymoon! Could it be that my checklist needed a serious overhaul? Surely not!

Did I pack my bags and head home? Of course not. You already know me better than that. I decided then and there to do yet another restart to make this relationship work! No one is perfect, and I was sure he would leave those things behind in order to build a better, stronger life together. Because we know that everyone changes for the better after they get married, right?

A NEW PATH

After practicing law for five years, my first instincts turned out to be correct. I was pretty sure that was *not* what I wanted to do for the rest of my life. But I certainly wasn't independently wealthy, so I was going to have to figure out something.

I was a good trial lawyer and loved being in court, but I didn't like all the hours spent alone in the library endlessly researching, writing, and revising. I would have two or three cases on the court's docket for the next week, so I would spend all weekend getting prepared for the one most likely to go to trial. Then, of course, that one would settle or get delayed, and the one I wasn't as prepared for would be called to trial.

I distinctly remember the pressure of having one hundred clients' files handed to me at my last firm. There is no way you can be up to speed on a hundred files, and I *despise* being unprepared, even though I'm pretty good at winging it.

I have a vivid memory of standing in court addressing the judge and feeling heart palpitations. I had to hold on to the edge of the chair to steady myself. I was only twenty-eight years old, and I *loved* speaking in court. I wasn't nervous at all; it was simply a manifestation of the mounting pressure I was under.

I also looked at the partners who were at the height of their careers, and they worked *even more* than I did. Even after being there for several years, I still saw my future becoming harder and more unpleasant. That's the point at which I knew it was time to pivot. I could have started counting the years to retirement and started waiting to die. But I knew if I was going to make a change, there was no better time than the present. We were still young, we didn't have children, and we only rented our home—so the timing for us was perfect.

But I strongly believe, no matter *what* your age, the best time to make a change is the minute you realize it's necessary. Procrastination is always tempting but never pays off.

I have read that the average person will change careers five to seven times over the course of their lives, and I have found this to be true in my own life. As I said at the beginning of this book, for better or worse, gone are the days of the gold watch retirement and the fat pension. We live in such a fast-changing world, so I expect career changes to happen even more frequently going forward. We *must* be nimble. We *must* observe what's going on around us and be perpetual students, ready to embrace the next big change that impacts our lives.

Of course, my mom knew the hours I was putting in and the pressure I was under, working as an attorney. She knew about the heart palpitations and was understandably concerned.

She, on the other hand, had started her own little business. That lady was *born* to be an entrepreneur! When I left home for college, she was completely at loose ends after raising her children, and she suddenly had nothing to fill her time. We lived on seven acres on Highway 59 in Marshall, Texas; and my brother Jimmy, and his wife Kay, and their sons Joshua and

Jacob, lived next door on a few acres. Their home had come with a little rental house, nothing fancy at all, but it did have highway frontage. So Jimmy, always a wheeler-dealer himself, came up with the idea for Kay and Mom to open a little "swap shop" in the building. He bought out a garage sale, which became their first load of inventory. A business owner was born!

My mom *loved* working in that shop. She and Kay would go to garage sales, estate sales, and antique auctions, and buy low and sell high—well, at least higher than they had paid. My mom was always a scrapper. One of her favorite finds was two pairs of coveralls at a garage sale that still had the tags on them! Of course, she took them straight back to JC Penney's, who gave her a $40 cash refund for them. In the early 1980s, that was a good day's work! She was incredulous that somebody had been too lazy to return them for cold, hard cash. Humbler beginnings you will never find than her little shop on the side of the highway. It was rent-free, however, so the price was right.

After just a few years, Kay phased out of the business, as she was getting really busy with her boys. So mom was on her own—queen of the swap shop!

Over the years, Mom worked a bit off and on with a woman who taught her that handmade quilts were a hot item and brought a hefty price tag. The only problem was the little ladies who made the quilts could only make one every couple of months, so it was hard to fill demand, and of course they were expensive.

This was around the time that imported quilts started arriving from China, so she found importers and began ordering wholesale. Now, so that this doesn't sound too fancy, she would find these quilts at department stores, look for the name and contact information of the manufacturer, and reach out about how to order. She shared with her siblings how popular quilts were, and soon her brother, Billy, went into the importing business directly when he saw how good the business could be. Her sister, my aunt Charmaine, started ordering quilts wholesale and selling them in Canton, Texas at the monthly Trade Days market. Then her kids started opening shops, as did most of the cousins.

I consider this a "family business" of sorts, but not in the sense most people think, meaning you were handed down a business, silver-spoon style. This family business was redneck style all the way! Other than my mom, who had her little shop on the highway, most family members were finding a good fit in tourist towns where shoppers were "hemmed up" walking and browsing in one area.

Shortly after I remarried, on a visit home to Marshall, Mom could tell I really wasn't happy being an attorney. She pulled out her pink clipboard with loose-leaf paper (I still have it!) and said, "Let me show you something. I make more money than you do! You don't have to be a lawyer."

So I approached my new husband with this harebrained idea. My mom showed him the money she was bringing in, but he was skeptical and said, "But we're *professionals*."

He was back in school at that point after having spent several years in the Marine Corps. She wasn't exactly blown away by *his* professional status! On the other hand, he wasn't really excited about the idea of running a swap shop on the side of the road after marrying an attorney.

It's easy for all of us to let pride and "keeping up appearances" get in the way of taking the actions needed to change our lives. I have watched too many people stay on an unhappy path because it sounded impressive. Walking away from my law career was a big risk, but I couldn't live with the alternative. Always one to make a backup plan, I believed I could return to the practice if I had to. But first, I had to take my best shot at getting out.

So that's what I did: I made the first major restart in my work life.

EVALUATE THE RISKS, THEN TAKE YOUR SHOT

Although I didn't yet know all the repercussions of making this first step toward change, it became a pretty big restart. It incorporated a new relationship, a new career—and, pretty soon, moving to a new town—all within the first year of our marriage. Even though there's always risk involved in making any change, and here I was making several major changes at once, I was open to it.

Of course it was difficult to make the decision to walk away from what people expected. I thought I would stay a lawyer forever because that's such a desired position. But once I really experienced it and looked at it realistically, I could confidently say, "I don't want this for my life."

I had to take that chance, for the possibility of something *better*.

I did consider the worst-case scenario, asking myself, "What's the worst thing that could happen, and how would I handle myself if it did?"

You have to mitigate your risk and say, "I'm going to do it. If it doesn't work out, I can always go back to what I did before or make another change." But then, at some point, you just have to take your shot.

You have to do whatever it takes to have hope for a better quality of life.

Now, don't get me wrong. Just because I didn't want to be a lawyer anymore didn't mean I didn't *work*. Once we started our own business, I worked way more hours, but I was working to build a life, to build some freedom, and to have more opportunities.

You have to have something ahead of you that you want to work toward. Look at the people who have "made it" in whatever area you are considering. If you don't like where those people are, where the path is leading you, and that's not a good life, then it's not worth staying on that path. If you see them and they've got the life you want, then that will give you the courage to continue.

So ask yourself: What are you doing? Why are you on this path?

And if it's not the right path for you, or it's not heading in the right direction for your life, then make a change. Period.

LEARNING TO "PO' BOY" IT

The following weekend, we scheduled a trip to visit my uncle in Branson, Missouri, where he had set up his wholesale quilt-importing headquarters and where his children were setting up shops. He had been a prominent executive in a large company in Shreveport, Louisiana and was at an age where he could retire. Yet, instead of taking it easy, he had moved his entire extended family to another state and made a total restart of his career, as well. I guess restarting runs in my family's blood!

During our visit, I noticed my husband was much more impressed with the cute, highly successful gift shops our Branson relatives were operating than he had been with my mom's swap shop. Understandably, the gift shops suited his image of what a "professional" would do for a career much better than my mom's little shop on the side of the road. It's funny that my mother was already earning more in that little shop—and working *far* fewer hours—than I was as an attorney, but I supposedly had the prestigious position. Forget prestige and get real! Cash on the barrelhead is worth a lot more than fancy titles. But my husband hadn't learned that lesson yet.

On that first visit, my uncle gave us some good, down-to-earth advice. He told us if we wanted to go into business, we had to be willing to "po' boy" it. We had to be willing to pour everything we could back into the business and live as cheaply as possible. I think most people have a romanticized view of being a business owner. Our reality was *very* different!

We knew we wanted to find a tourist town to open our business, but that took money—something we had very little of. My husband's father was an astute businessman who, among other ventures, owned several coin-operated car washes in and around Lubbock, Texas. One was in the little town of Post with a population of 4,000. It was about an hour from Lubbock, but it was the only town with a stoplight on the five-hour drive between Lubbock and Dallas, and his car wash was right by that stoplight. As luck would have it, that carwash included a little rundown building, about 600 square feet, that his dad had just been using for storage. He said that if we put the sweat equity into cleaning it up, we could use it rent-free, since it had just been thrown in as a bonus when he bought the car wash.

We would also need a cheap place to live, and luckily my father-in-law had just bought a 1965 Avion trailer—a knockoff Airstream—for a few thousand dollars. He didn't really have a use for it, but it had been a good deal and really helped out the guy he bought it from. It didn't have plumbing hookups, but we were able to park it right behind the shop, where they added a *very* small bathroom with a toilet and tiny shower. Sure, we had to go into the shop at night if we wanted to use the bathroom, but that was a small sacrifice for becoming our own bosses! We were really living large.

So, father and son fixed up the little shop and built some poles on which we could hang our display quilts to catch travelers' eyes as they drove down the highway and lure customers into the shop. I sold my cool Mitsubishi sports car that I loved, and after I paid off the loan, we had about $7,500 to buy our first load of inventory. We placed a couple of orders, with my mom's suggestions to maximize our investment. Then she brought us a nice load of some of her back stock of bestsellers that she didn't have to pay for yet and said we could pay her as we were able.

We cut neon index cards in quarters and pinned them onto the quilts as our price tags, because that's the way my mom did it in her shop. We would write the name of the pattern, the price, a vendor code, and a backward number to tell us what we paid for the quilt in case we needed to negotiate—weren't we so sophisticated? We also set up plug-in lights to shine up on the quilts so we could stay open at night. Let's face it: we were in no rush each night to go into the bathroom-less Avion trailer!

On November 3, 1995, we were officially ready to open for business.

We were really ambitious. The town had recently opened up a monthly Trades Days market, following the trend of some other small Texas towns. On opening day, we had a booth at Trades Days, manned by my husband, while I was running the shop in town. I couldn't help but notice that I was working longer hours than ever before, but I felt so free! It didn't feel like work at all because it was all for *our* business.

We were really fortunate the little shop did well right from the start. It was close to Christmastime when we opened, so I didn't have time to order a lot of Christmas items. The demand for things like quilted tree skirts and little gifts and stocking stuffers was really high. My mom used to reminisce in later years, "You could sell *anything* in the nineties." And we did.

We would sell the few tree skirts we had, and then we would make a run to Lubbock, to discount stores like TJ Maxx and Marshalls, where we would buy quilted tree skirts for around $15. Then we'd remove the retail store's tags, price them for $45, and sell them like hotcakes. I remember once having to get them out of my trunk, yanking off those Marshalls' tags, while customers waited eagerly inside our shop!

In November of 1995, we grossed almost $20,000 in that tiny

little store. We were averaging a profit margin more than triple our cost, so we profited around $14,000 in that first month, which enabled us to pay my mom for all the quilts she'd brought us, as well as to invest the rest in more inventory. We did go out to eat at the little burger joint and the Mexican restaurant as our only splurges. You couldn't really cook in the Avion trailer, after all.

In December, we grossed about $35,000, if you can believe it.

Then I started looking around, ready to get out of dodge. I was grateful for this great start for our business, but now it was time to move to a proper tourist town!

CHAPTER 6

====

MY CAREER EVOLUTION

The top tourist area in Texas was and is Fredericksburg, right in the middle of the state. Some of my cousins had considered moving there to open stores but turned it down because, being a German town, they had the limiting belief that tourists would all want German-made items. Not true at all.

I was getting concerned because my husband was thinking about putting down roots in Post, Texas and was starting to look at houses there—but there was no way I was going to spend my life or raise a family in Post! The town had really taken us in, and we had quickly made some great friends, but I couldn't picture a life personally that involved raising my future children in such a small town. Such a small, *flat*, West Texas town.

Since I had no intention of staying in Post, I could see that we needed to start making plans to get out of town sooner than later. I had already requested information from the Fredericksburg Chamber of Commerce, and they sent us demographics about the town, tourism, and the housing market. More than ever, I was convinced that Fredericksburg was going to be the place for us. He was not as convinced.

One night, we were keeping the quilt shop open late and having quite a disagreement about whether to move or stay put. A man walked in, having been lured by the lighted quilts. After looking for a few minutes, he said, "This sure is a cute shop. You know what this reminds me of? Fredericksburg. Y'all should have a shop in Fredericksburg!"

My husband was *not* ready for another restart quite so soon, but even *he* couldn't fight against it at that point. So he started begrudgingly calling that man the "Fredericksburg angel."

In January of 1996, I kept the shop in Post open while my husband and his dad went down to scout out Fredericksburg, about five hours away. Even they had to admit that the town was definitely popping with action! Tourists had discovered Fredericksburg over the past few years, and the town was so full, as mom said, "you couldn't stir 'em with a stick." The only problem was there were very few retail spaces available to rent. In fact, the only one they found was a little old house on the very far west end of Main Street. It wasn't anything fancy, but neither was our place in Post, and we were doing just fine. The rent was $900 per month, which didn't seem too bad, so we signed a lease and started preparing to move.

Remember, when starting a business, you *must* be willing to "po' boy it." We couldn't afford to rent a house or apartment, since every extra dime needed to go right back into inventory. It only made sense to live in the quilt shop. It was a house, after all, and it did have a big, king-size bed in the front room for displaying our quilts. And let's face it: it was a big step up from the Avion trailer; at least the bathroom was inside!

We found a woman in Post who could run the store there while we made the move to Fredericksburg. In most businesses, you'll find that you aren't completely replaceable. The sales definitely dipped after we left, but it was still something to keep us going while we worked to open in the new town. And our expenses in Post were so low that there was no reason not to keep it open.

I still remember vividly our little moving trailer, a converted boat-hauling trailer, stacked probably eight feet high with all our worldly possessions. We definitely looked like "country come to town." You have to be willing to be humble when it's time for a restart, starting from the bottom and slowly working up.

GRAND OPENING

We moved into the little shop in Fredericksburg and started getting ready for our opening. My mom and aunt were so excited about the expansion that they came down to help us, and to bring another load of quilts from my mom's supply. They were buying out all the popular "Boot" quilts (white quilts with red and blue cowboy boots appliquéd all over them) that they could find in department stores. We were selling them for four times the price! Good old American free enterprise at work.

We knew we needed a location down in the main walking area of Fredericksburg. Rents were much higher, but everyone in the family who had stores had encouraged us to rent the best location we could find. Location is just as important in retail as in residential real estate! I remember driving around the cute tourist towns of Branson and Eureka Springs, Arkansas, with our uncle. We would see a cute building on a side street, out of the main traffic pattern, and he would say, "You see that? That's what you call a good place to starve."

We knew we needed a "golden blocks" location eventually, but we were also happy to keep one that was a little farther out. Others in the family had found that having two different kinds of shops attracted two kinds of customers. We often sold quilts to those driving down Highway 290 (also Fredericksburg's Main Street) because they saw them hanging outside. They were driving across state or even across several states and didn't even know Fredericksburg existed. They never would have fought for a parking place to stop at a store in the crowded downtown area.

My husband and his father attempted to find a downtown location, with no luck. They were told we could be added to a waiting list for a gorgeous store in an amazing location, but that we would be "way down" on the list. That shop was renting for *$8,000 a month* in 1996! When I showed my mom and my aunt "Mimi," as I have always called her, around the bustling downtown area of Fredericksburg, we walked past one store that had signs in the window saying "40 percent off everything!" With her typical, common-sense wisdom, my mom said, "Stores don't offer 40 percent off everything unless they're going out of business. Let's go talk to them."

We walked in and met the owner, and she said, yes, they owned the building but intended to close their store to focus on their bed and breakfast business. They had even sold a few of the same quilt lines we carried and acknowledged it was a good business. She agreed to rent us this tiny but cute little 600-square-foot space for $1,900 per month.

My husband was still in the Marine Reserve at this time, which paid about $300 per month and required him to go for "drill" one weekend per month. When you are making a restart, every $300 counts! He was away at drill when we found this rental opportunity, so I called to ask what he thought we should do. This was a huge opportunity to get a store in the golden blocks, even if on the very edge, but we would now be opening *two* stores at the same time! Having only been open for less than three months total, we were about to have three stores all at once!

To his credit, he didn't flinch. He said, "Absolutely! We have to get that location." His certainty took me aback a little, but it was also encouraging. It definitely took the pressure off of me, and I'll always appreciate that moment as being pivotal in getting our business really off the ground.

My mom and I then went to a bank to see about opening a line of credit. They reviewed our financials and said they thought they could help, especially since I was a lawyer. That came in handy many times in those early years. Bankers especially liked it because they figured I would go back to practicing law before I would default on a loan or mortgage. Of course they were right—but thank goodness I never had to.

Then my mom sprung one of her classic lines. The banker said they didn't foresee a problem issuing the line of credit; they would just need to see a profit-and-loss statement. She leaned over, looked at him straight on and said, "Oh, it's all profit. There ain't no loss."

We opened the west store in February and had the downtown store open by my birthday on March 6. Traffic was modest the first few days, and we couldn't help but feel just a twinge of anxiety. But then, a few days later, we learned a quick lesson about what spring break means for business in Fredericksburg. It was as if a switch had been flipped, and we suddenly had *two* shops hustling and bustling in our new town—in addition to the one in Post!

My husband would drive me the mile and a half to the downtown store in the morning, drop me off, then return to work in the slower shop where we also lived. Between the two of us, I was the natural salesperson, so it only made sense that I work in the busier store.

Oh, the hours we worked! But what an exhilarating sense of freedom.

One day, soon after we moved to town, the little old man who lived next door showed us how to plant potatoes in his backyard. During one of these planting sessions, I saw some customers drive up, so I ran inside, sold them a quilt, and just a few minutes later was back outside planting potatoes. I made as much on that one quilt sale as I would have practicing law for a day, and the rest of the day was mine to learn new things. That was so many years ago, but I remember the feeling of freedom—of really *living* life—so clearly.

I also remember the weekends that my husband had to go to

Dallas for drill, taking our only car, a Ford Taurus, with him. We had one car and two shops—and only *me* to keep the busier one open, since we didn't have employees yet. When he was gone, I would just *walk* the mile and a half from the west end shop where we slept to the shop downtown. Because that was the busier location, if we only opened one, it had to be that one. Walking the mile and a half wasn't too bad, but it probably looked a little ridiculous, because I would restock the quilts I had sold the day before by loading as many new quilts as I could carry from our extra supply into a black garbage bag and head out with it slung across my shoulder.

Remember that when you are a real entrepreneur, you're never "too good" to do what needs to be done. Your drive to succeed will overshadow any fear that someone might see you hauling quilts in a garbage bag without a car. It just doesn't matter. At that moment, having that popular quilt replaced in stock so I could sell it again was all that mattered!

Within just a few months, we were able to hire a few employees, mostly older ladies we met in church who wanted a little extra spending money. That gave us a little room to breathe and to keep an eye out for the next opportunity to come our way.

MAKE A DECISION AND KEEP MOVING

I really like the saying, "I either win or I learn." I don't know about you, but almost everything I know, I learned by doing it the wrong way first.

Think of life as a video game. You don't pick up a detailed manual and read and study up on how to play the game and advance to the next level. You pick up the controller and start crashing into things. Then you back up and try again. You crash again, but in a different way this time. Each crash teaches you what doesn't work. Each time you advance teaches you what does work.

So why is everyone so afraid to make a mistake? If a gamer wants to be sure not to crash, the best way is to sit in neutral, afraid to move. Unfortunately, that is also the best way to guarantee you will never advance and never win. I read a quote recently that said, "The only risk is not taking a risk." Sitting on the sidelines, afraid to try, is a good way to live a very dull, unfulfilling life. I've often heard that when people are nearing the end of life, they mostly regret all the chances they *didn't* take and the things they *didn't* try.

Once I decided my best shot at a happy life with at least a little autonomy was to walk away from practicing law and start my own business, it was full steam ahead! Many people would have spent months, if not years, developing a business plan and researching every last detail of their upcoming move. I recall family members who had also decided to open up quilt shops in different areas driving all over the country looking for the perfect location. One searched for nearly a year before finding "the" spot. What was the value of an entire *year* of lost revenue? And did they find the perfect place? Not really. A few years later, after some failures and some successes, they were out of the business altogether. My point is follow your gut, take your shot, and see where it leads you. The paralysis caused by overanalysis is deadly and certainly not a way to start off a new phase with momentum!

EYE FOR OPPORTUNITY

Our second business came to be the way all of them have: no business plan, no long-range plan—just a passion that grew into something more.

I have always loved real estate; I find potential in every house I see. Of course, investing in real estate takes capital, or creativity, and I always had a lot more creativity than capital. I've also always kept up with real estate prices as a hobby. I wanted to start purchasing rental properties in Fredericksburg as soon as we moved there, but property prices were always so expensive. Long-term renters simply couldn't pay the rental prices I would have had to charge just to cover the mortgage.

Fortunately, Fredericksburg has long been known for its bed and breakfast industry. There were a few traditional inns, like you might picture, where everyone comes together for breakfast. But far more common were the little cottages around town, sometimes on their own lot, sometimes in someone's backyard. Our town truly did have many Airbnb's before that company even existed. I looked into the vacation-rental market and learned that you could bring in far more rental revenue than in long-term rentals. This gave me hope for being able to successfully invest in real estate in Fredericksburg. It only made sense, of course, to start small, on property we already owned.

After living in our quilt shop for a few months, *sleeping in the display bed*, we learned that I was pregnant with our first daughter, Savannah. I didn't see how we could keep living in the shop with a baby, so we started looking for a house. Typically, when you are self-employed, as we now were, you have to have been in business at least two years to get a mortgage. We had only been in business for around eight months when we first spoke to the mortgage company. But once again my law degree came in handy, and they agreed to give us a loan, figuring that I could always practice law if we needed additional income. We bought a cute little three-bedroom, two-bath house in a slightly older neighborhood. It was around $150,000, which seemed like a lot for Texas in 1996.

Our house was perfectly comfortable, and we had both our daughters while living in that home. Savannah Jeannine was born in April of 1997, and Sealy Elizabeth was born in June of 1998. You may wonder why my two children were born only fourteen months apart. Savannah was born when I was thirty. I told my doctor we might want to have three or four children, so he told me I'd need to have the next one right away to minimize the risk of having them past the age of thirty-five.

Savannah was a delightful little baby, always laughing and sleeping through the night from the age of five weeks.

Then we had Sealy. She was not delightful. She was a colicky, crying nightmare for several months! So, after having her, I told the doctor, "Turns out we're good with just the two!"

A lot can change in just over a year when you are fearlessly chasing your dream and are willing to work very, very hard and make a lot of sacrifices along the way. Just nineteen months earlier, we had been living in an old Avion trailer with no bathroom inside; and now we had three stores and this house that was nearly new and in great condition, and two beautiful baby girls. We couldn't believe our luck, honestly.

As nice as our little starter family home was, I've always had a love of old houses. In 1999, I started looking seriously for an old, historic home for our family to grow up in. There was very little available on the market and nothing exciting. So I stopped by the office of a financial advisor who lived and worked from her gorgeous turn-of-the-century, two-story home, and I asked if she had ever considered selling. She told me her grandfather had built that home, so she didn't foresee ever selling. But she also mentioned a woman in town who had divorced a few years ago. The woman was recently remarried to a man who lived in another town, and she was likely going to decide to sell soon.

I jumped in my car and drove straight there. The home clearly needed a lot of TLC, but the bones were amazing, with lots of original Victorian detail, including a turret in the corner. No one was home, so I left a note on the door stating that I had an interest in buying the home. The owner was out of town with her new husband, but as it turned out, her mother was staying in the house and relayed the message. I had looked on the appraisal district site already and saw that the house was around 2,600 square feet, built in 1910, and had three bedrooms, two bathrooms, a formal dining room, plus a breakfast room, a formal living room, *and* a den. I was sold already!

It had original knob-and-tube wiring in most of the house and had *never* had central heat and air. But when the owner called me and said she wouldn't take less than $200,000 for it, I was ready to leap on it! My husband, not so much. Like a lot of men, he wasn't thrilled about leaving the comfort of our new house for the inconvenience of an old house. Fortunately, we were financially able to stay in our current home for the eight months it took to completely renovate the house. The renovation was quite a success, and we were featured on the 1999 Christmas Home Tour benefiting the local historic society.

OPEN TO WHERE THE ROAD LED US

A short while later, we decided to undertake renovation of the detached garage on the side of the property, which would have been the original carriage house. Little did we know where that project would take us!

The little building was termite-ridden and had a dirt floor, but it was already built in the setback; that meant it was built too close to the road according to today's code. Since it was old, we couldn't be forced to move it. This mattered, because if we moved it away from the street in compliance with current codes, it would be in the middle of our backyard, wasting space. As long as we renovated it where it stood, it could remain in that location. Let me tell you, that was one thorough renovation. Basically, every piece of wood was replaced due to termite damage and wood rot, and the entire building had to be lifted to pour a foundation. We even had to expand the footprint to add a bath, which technically shouldn't have been allowed. Nonetheless, we now had a really pretty little guesthouse on the property rather than a falling-down garage.

The renovation, however, cost *way* more than we expected—to the tune of $80,000—and we felt that was too big an investment for grandma to stay in once or twice a year. So, we decided to dip our toe into the bed and breakfast rental pool. That one little renovated cottage changed our business forever. Restart!

We were naturally wary of renting out a cottage that was so

close to our home. I'm not sure we would have had the nerve to try, were it not for the woman who rented us that first downtown store and who also ran a bed-and-breakfast reservation service. She was willing to take us on a trial basis to see if we liked it. Once again, we saw an opportunity and were willing to take a risk, but we had a backup plan. If we absolutely hated it, she was willing to let us remove it from the rental pool.

We gave it a try and loved it. We started bringing in a couple thousand extra dollars per month, and we very rarely saw the guests. We were hooked!

A few months later, we purchased a cottage just a few blocks away and started booking it, as well. Over time, we were able to buy the two cottages across the street and add them to our collection.

A THIRD (AND FOURTH) BUSINESS IS BORN

After successfully opening a few little cottages, I felt we might be ready to take on a bigger property.

As luck would have it, a historic rock inn came up for sale in a great location downtown. It had six suites and was listed for sale for under $600,000 after a few price drops. I knew it was a steal, but there was no way I could come up with a 20-30 percent down payment, which commercial lenders were requiring. So, I made a call to a more aggressive banker I had recently met and asked him if the seller agreed to carry the down payment— meaning that we would make payments to the seller instead of coming up with all of the down payment at once—would the bank consider making the loan? He got together with the committee and said if we could come up with 10 percent and the seller would carry 30 percent, the bank would finance the remaining 60 percent.

Since the purchase of our first little starter home, we had been using the same realtor. Back in the old days, people would see a real estate office sign and just walk in off the street. Whoever met us at the door would be our agent, and we were pretty well stuck with them for life for better or worse. You know how hard it is to break up with your hairdresser? Breaking up with your real estate agent is just as hard! There was no internet to research reviews and make a choice about this person who would become such a lasting part of our lives. The fellow who met us at the door that day was a very kind man. He and his wife even babysat our daughters a time or two. But he was one of those agents who thought the way he could best represent our interests was to *fight* for us, which often led to turning off the other side. His every instinct, when it came to sales, was wrong. I recall having one of our vacation rentals listed for sale with him. After a showing one Saturday morning, he told us that the potential buyers really liked it and were impressed with the revenue it was generating. He then reassured us, "Don't worry, though; I told them y'all were really good at this B&B stuff, and they shouldn't think they were going to do as well as y'all." My inner salesperson cringed completely!

So on this particular deal, I decided to go straight to the owner, bypassing our agent altogether as far as the negotiation phase. I didn't have a license, so I could talk to anyone I pleased. I met her at McDonald's and went over my proposal. She was ready to move on, so after a little back and forth going over the details with her grown children, she decided to do the deal. I wrote out all the terms and handed it to our agent, saying as nicely as I could, "Just write it up this way. Don't fight for us and don't ask for anything extra."

After that deal closed, I recall thinking I did *all* the work so he could make a $17,000 commission, and he had the nerve to give me a little tub of body butter as a closing gift. (Tip: based on the value of the sale, if you're going to give a really cheap closing gift, you're *far* better off giving nothing at all!) I decided I needed to sever the relationship with our realtor—but, being a good Southern girl, I didn't want to hurt anyone's feelings. I figured the perfect solution was to get my own license. That way, he couldn't take offense when I didn't use him anymore!

I got my real estate license in 2009, just for my own deals at that time. This would come in *really* handy in a few years, when I decided to start a real estate team with my new husband Wes (but I'm getting ahead of myself again!).

LET'S OPEN A RESERVATION SERVICE, TOO!

Restarting does not have to mean going in completely new directions. Sometimes, it involves simply adding services or businesses to what you are already doing. You already have expertise in your current field, so it is really helpful not to need to reinvent the wheel.

Our vacation rental portfolio was growing pretty large, and with the additional six-suite traditional inn on the west end of Main we were renovating, we were about to have a whopping twenty-six rooms available for rent. Paying the rental commission on all of those rooms cut into our profit margin considerably, so we had no choice but to consider taking our own reservations. I had never wanted to leave our booking company, but with that many rooms, the model was simply changing for us. Booking your own place is a *big* undertaking, but since we had retail stores, we already had physical office spaces on Main Street, employees, computers, and telephones; why *wouldn't* we take our own reservations?

Before this obvious new path could become a reality, however, I had to do something very difficult—something I dreaded to my core. Our friend and former landlord in the first downtown store was the one who encouraged us to open our first cottage and let her rent it. Our cottages had become a large part of her portfolio. She had even joked in the past that I'd better not ever leave them. Of course, I had said I wouldn't, as I had zero plans or even a desire to take our own reservations at the time.

But life happens. Business models change. And the time had come where I absolutely knew the right thing for our business and my family was to take our own reservations. I knew that telling her would be an awful blow, and I genuinely regretted that it was going to cause her difficulties. But in the long run, you do what you have to do. Even though it was over fifteen years ago, I remember it like it was yesterday. I stepped outside of our store and walked the three agonizing blocks to her office and broke the news. As I feared, it was like a gut punch to her business. I volunteered to let her take reservations at the same time we did for a few months so she could phase us out less painfully while hopefully picking up some other rooms.

Then she did what a lot of people do and cut off her nose to spite her face. She said, "The day you take your first booking, we won't book for you anymore." I certainly couldn't blame her, but I learned two things in that encounter. First, don't let emotions make your business decisions; and second, don't ever become so dependent on one property owner, one lead source, or even one person, that their decision to leave you can bring you to such a tough place. And I never have.

Unfortunately, I was reminded in that encounter that growth almost always includes some amount of pain and discomfort. If you aren't willing to walk through it, you can't grow.

Once the decision had been made, and the news had been broken, I knew I would need a few more things to get started. First, I would need a beautiful website and great photography of our rooms. As you can probably guess, I had already started attending B&B conferences to learn more since I'm such a big believer in always knowing your craft better than anyone else. I had met vendors in both the website and photography spaces, so I was able to choose a web designer pretty quickly. They confirmed what I already knew: getting high-quality photos would be key to making the website beautiful and successful. I reached out to the top photography group, the best in the B&B business. Amazingly, they had a yearlong wait and would cost about $19,000 for the initial set of photography. They were extremely gracious, however, and encouraged me to do it myself. They said, "Your properties are going to need updated photos regularly, so as you grow, it only makes sense to bring the photography in-house."

Taking the bull by the horns once again, I purchased $5,000 worth of professional DSLR camera equipment, enrolled in a one-week photography course, and started my new sub-career.

Over the years, I took many courses and bought a lot more equipment. My skill level grew dramatically, but I never learned to love photography. I was ecstatic when the day came where I didn't have to do the photos myself any longer, but I did it as long as it took until we could afford to pay someone.

The other thing I needed was a really organized manager to help me run this completely new business. I was talking about it at the dance studio one day where my daughters were taking dance class, and my dear friend and fellow dance mom, Tami Smith, volunteered. "Hire me! I'm sick of driving thirty minutes to Kerrville every day for work!"

She was and is one of the most organized, intelligent people I have ever met, so it didn't take me long to make that decision! Tami said her only concern was that she was afraid she would get bored, and she wondered why I would always laugh when she said that. She has been running Absolute Charm Reservation Service since 2007 and counting, and she says she hasn't had a boring day yet!

CHANGE JUST KEEPS COMING

These years were all about change. We went from one store to two stores to three stores quickly—and up to, at one point, six stores. And we looked around and saw an opening, an opportunity, to get into the B&B business, then real estate, and then a reservation service. We were on a *journey*, and the path we followed had so many twists and turns. Spoiler alert: we will always be on a journey, and the twists and turns just keep coming! That's how we know we are alive.

I think most people, especially the younger they are, see everything as a destination. But I don't think you reach a destination until you die. Instead, I think of life like a long interstate. It has all these off- and on-ramps; as you try different things, you're getting on, you're getting off, and then getting back on the interstate. You're adjusting and making sure that's still the path you want. "No, let's take this highway." Or, "I'm tired of the interstate. Let's take the back road. This will be a better part of life."

When on earth do we ever arrive? We don't, because we're constantly going.

And in this world, change is the one thing we all know is inevitable; it's never just going to be a one-time change. Things are going to keep changing.

Even after we had the shops in Fredericksburg, we started bringing in other things to test, like women's clothing and baby clothing. People really liked it, but we had to be open to that change, and it was hard. My manager and friend Tami said, "Clothing scares me; you know, sizing scares me. How do we know what to get?"

I acknowledged her fear and said, "I know, but we can't be scared. What we should be scared of is *not* changing. Because we will die if we don't change."

So we kept testing, experimenting, and we grew that business up. Later, however, after we owned some of our own B&Bs and had the B&B reservation service, in addition to retail and real estate, I realized something was going to have to give. We had to be realistic about which of those businesses was requiring the most of us while providing us with the least. The time came when retail took the most out of us: the most time and the most mental energy, while giving the least profit. And I didn't like the future of retail. So I had to make hard decisions.

We had to cut away things. You can't always just add; sometimes you have to be willing to cut away something. We couldn't do justice to the B&B service and become number one in real estate in town, *and* run retail also.

So sometimes being willing to take on and grow means being willing to prune and not look at it as a failure, but as a beautiful evolution of where those off-ramps are leading you. It's just that winding path that life is intended to be. Don't beat yourself up when things don't work out or you have to make changes. Just enjoy taking that journey, making every little path you take a little better than the one before.

WORKING *HARD*, EVEN WITH HELP

Tami wanted to give thirty days' notice to her previous job, which was very noble, but left me *extremely* shorthanded as I launched the reservation company. When we got started, I worked *seventy-five days* in a row without a day off. That's the kind of thing you definitely remember! But I also knew it would be hard to train someone to do a job that really hadn't even been created yet, so I had to dive in with both feet to figure out what to say on the phone to guests, how to use the reservation software, and how to arrange for cleaning and breakfast.

Those were some long, hard days. My mom, who was seventy-eight at the time, tried to help out; and so did the quilt salespeople, since we were operating out of our retail space. Even my little daughter, Savannah—who was ten at the time—jumped in and did her best. Luckily this was in the summer, so she was out of school. She was actually an amazing helper, competently taking reservations over the phone. Desperate times call for desperate measures, and she has always been an entrepreneurial beast. At the time, my mom just shook her head and said, "All you have is old ladies and little girls to help you!"

We managed to get up and running successfully, but soon after Tami Smith started working, she noticed we were booking so well that she spent most of her time on the phone saying, "I'm sorry, but we're full."

A few of our friends started asking if we would represent their properties as well. It had not been our intention to build a full-fledged reservation service, but by creating a great website that could take real-time bookings, we were able to create demand for our services.

Once that train leaves the station, it *will* take on a life of its own, much of which you cannot foresee at first. Do you see a pattern here? Many, perhaps most, businesses are born out of a need that arises as you go along. Do what you do at a high level, always exceed expectations, and others will notice and want to join you. We did, and right then and there, another business was born!

We currently represent roughly 200 rooms or cottages and have a very strong reservation business. That business now has four full-time reservationists, in addition to Tami Smith, the manager, as well as a full housekeeping division which employs dozens of people. It not only provided jobs for many people, but it has also created enough ongoing revenue to allow us to create our *next* business: the real estate business.

CHAPTER 7

RESTART #3: STARTING OVER AT FORTY-SEVEN

Life and business continued along. We added quilt shop retail locations; we added vacation rentals of our own; and we added properties to our reservation service, as well.

While my work life was going well, my husband and I separated in September of 2013. He's a good person, but the marriage just wasn't working at all. We were married, but I didn't have a husband.

People often ask me why I didn't leave sooner, and I usually say there were two factors. First, I didn't think the business could financially withstand being cut in two at that point, and I had to make sure there was enough money to take care of myself and the girls. Second, I didn't want the girls to *have* to spend every first, third, and fifth weekend away from me at that stage of life. I waited until they were about old enough to drive; that way, they could spend all the time they wanted with him—after all, he only moved a mile away—but if things weren't as they should be, they could leave. They were old enough to make their own choices, and the judge wouldn't force them to spend time with *anyone* against their will.

There is a third reason I didn't leave my marriage earlier, and it may be the biggest reason: while he and I did not have a "real" marriage at this point, he was never abusive to any of us in any way. He always attended the girls' dance competitions and pageants and school plays and was very supportive of them in all they did. He had a good sense of humor and was enjoyable to talk to. If that had not been the case, the first two reasons would not have mattered, and we would have left.

As often happens in cases like this, I suddenly became much more appealing to him after I didn't want him anymore. I guess that's just human nature. After just a few weeks of peace, he started to pursue me...in his way, at least. At this point, I did not want to go back. But what *really* helped me get through this time was the girls. They said, "If he comes back home, we will leave." While they loved their dad tremendously, they knew he and I shouldn't be married. More than anything, the two of them helped me stay strong enough to do what needed to be done.

The time of separation as we moved toward divorce was actually a very liberating and peaceful time for me. After eighteen years of marriage, I still cared for him and wanted him to be safe and sound, but I knew it was over. Having spent a few months alone in the house with the girls had just reinforced for me that I was doing what was best.

He didn't see it that way at the time and began to dig in deeper as the process moved along. He pulled out all the stops, even getting the judge to require us to go to counseling yet again. So we went, but of course nothing changed. At that point, my mind was made up and I just needed my ticket punched. I felt his real concern was not actually losing me as a person, as a wife, but losing the security and lifestyle, the normalcy, that having me around provided. And I had finally decided that it wasn't going to be good enough for me anymore. I thought back to what Sealy had asked me months before: "Is this it for you?" I had my answer. It was not. I wanted so much more out of life.

It also reminded me of what the counselor told me when my first husband left: that I wasn't mourning a life with *him,* but mourning my vision of what that life would have been. I think the same can be said for the girls' dad. We didn't have enough between us for him to actually mourn losing me; I believe he was simply mourning the change.

EVERY RESTART IS DIFFERENT

I know I've said my first divorce was my hardest restart—and in many ways, it truly was because it was the *first.* But he and I weren't together for very long, and we didn't have kids to tie us together. He almost feels like an ex-boyfriend—someone I just dated a long time ago.

My second divorce, on the other hand, felt like a much more significant situation. After all, we built these businesses and had these two wonderful girls together. I still remember sitting at the kitchen table and him just crying, which was unusual for him; he was crying in fear of what his life would be like. It was not what he wanted, and that was scary. He wasn't scared of losing me; he was frightened of the *change*. Isn't that such a normal human emotion?

I sat with him, but my eyes were dry. I'd cried many times in the eighteen years of our marriage; by then, my tears were gone.

I remember my mom warning him when we got married, "If she ever stops crying, you'd better watch out. Be careful how you treat her, because it's like putting ashes on the coals of love— eventually it's just gone and there's no getting it back. When respect goes out the window, love is right behind it."

Most of all, this restart was just *different.* In some ways, it was harder than my first; in other ways, it was easier—mainly because, by that point in my life, I had realized that perfection was not going to happen. Living a perfect life is just a fantasy we have when we are younger.

All restarts are clearly not created equal. I've learned through the years that some are very painful, whereas others are joyous and amazing seasons of rejuvenation. No matter what type of restart you are facing, or will face, tackle it head-on with the full knowledge and faith that you have the tools to move through it and on to the next beautiful chapter of your life.

When it came to this divorce, once the decision was made, and once I came to grips with the idea I would now officially be a twice-divorced woman, it was like I was literally being reborn. I had to accept that facing that stigma, that sense of failure, was not enough to keep me down or hold me back.

I recognized that I was forty-seven, and I still had a chance to have a real life, to start over. Before, there were times when I realize now that I was sitting down, waiting to die. There were times when it did feel hopeless. There were times when I thought about leaving—but cutting our businesses in half could have destroyed them, and that was a chance I could not take. So, I made the hard decisions, and I just bucked up and focused on work and the kids.

But, of course, you can't fix something that someone else doesn't want to fix. There were times when it felt dark and hopeless and like it would never end. When the marriage ended, I felt like a butterfly coming out of a cocoon. It was a hard-fought and painful restart, but it was also quite wonderful. And not just for me. Whether he realized it or not, I was not what he truly wanted. And being someone's security blanket just wasn't enough for me any longer.

MOVING ON, AGAIN

We went to mediation to try to figure out how to divide up the businesses. If you are a realtor or in any type of business for very long, you know there is never enough money. You could always use more, and cutting the business in two hardly seems possible. At the time, we had two retail stores, the reservation service, plus a few B&B properties of our own.

I offered to transfer one of the businesses solely to him. He must not have thought he could run it, or he didn't want to. Let's face it: not everyone is crazy enough to want the fast-paced work schedule and stress that go hand in hand with being an entrepreneur. It just wasn't for him. To my surprise, and with the help of a great mediator, we were able to agree to a business buyout with a payment plan. It was a hefty amount, but I *always* believed in my ability to rebuild and rise from the ashes. If this was the price for my freedom, for this much-needed restart, I would find a way to pay it.

He was very distraught at the mediation, and my heart went out to him as a human being and as a friend. But I could see the light by now and just knew I had to keep moving toward it. I'm sure he truly was upset about all he was losing—daily time with his kids, his comfortable lifestyle, the knowledge that I was always there to make things work out. But it wasn't love. Not for me. And I believe not for him, either.

While my first restart was the most jarring, this was the *biggest restart* of my entire life. At forty-seven, this was my time to decide to give up and live out my days in a situation that was comfortable enough but not amazing enough for *either* of us—or to run like the wind. I could start waiting to die, or I could make the scary decision to take charge of my life and start living again.

I took my moment, and I've never looked back.

I've never wished him ill. Never. In fact, I hope he continues to find new happiness and a fulfilled life. Since that time, we have found a good place. A place of friendship. He often joins our family for holiday dinners, and he even spent a recent family vacation with us as we flew across the world to celebrate our daughter's wedding in Bora Bora.

The two best things to come out of the marriage were our

daughters and our businesses. As far as business, I feel I did a lot of the "heavy lifting," but he did one very important thing: he never got in the way. That may sound like I am minimizing his contribution, but I'm not. Just think about how hard it must be to jump off an entrepreneurial cliff with someone when that's not really part of your own nature. He absolutely could have held me back at any point. I'm sure I would have at least *tried* to slow down my growth and expansion dreams had he insisted. He always believed in my business ability and gave me a lot of encouragement and leeway. I'll always appreciate that and acknowledge it as a big part of what allowed me to accomplish whatever I have.

Obviously, our children are the greatest blessing either of us will ever know. Despite our differences, we never used our daughters as pawns, as so many people do. We never tried to put the kids in the middle of the situation; nor did we let them play one parent against the other—something I'm sure most kids try to pull when their parents divorce.

Shortly after the divorce, I recall dropping our younger daughter Sealy off at school, just before she got her driver's license. We were running behind, and she didn't want to walk in late; so she just wanted to ride around until next period, maybe go get coffee. I had a lot on my plate that morning, so I told her she would just have to go in late. She got out of the car and slammed the door.

Well that was *not* okay!

I rolled down the window and told her to figure out her own ride home. A few minutes later, I received a call from her father saying he was checking to see if everything was okay. He had just received a call from her asking for a ride home after school. He said it seemed odd, since I always drove her. He wanted to be sure something fishy wasn't going on. I explained the situation and told him it would be fine for him to pick her up.

As soon as school was over, my phone rang. It was Sealy apologizing for her behavior. Her dad had told her what she did was wrong and that he would take her home—but first, she needed to call and apologize. If more divorced parents, or even *married* parents, would respond the way he did that day, we would all have better kids.

TURNING THE CORNER

Our divorce was final on July 2, 2014, the day before my friend and manager Tami Smith, and her two daughters, my two daughters, and I left for a month-long trip to Europe, covering ten countries. That was the most amazing time of renewal and of feeling that I could do anything! I have never felt so free, so light and happy, as the day the six of us flew out on our girls' trip, completely unfettered. Some of my restarts had felt scary or overwhelming. This one felt natural, like a complete rebirth! I knew in my heart that we would *all* be okay.

Travel has long been an absolute obsession for me. We owe a debt of gratitude to Tami's husband Ken, who was willing to stay back and let all six of us girls head out across the pond on our own. What an exhilarating month that was! We took planes, trains, and automobiles (literally) all over Europe, all centered around unique experiences. We learned to make macarons in a private class in Paris. We learned to row traditional boats in Venice. We learned how to get a French-made stick-shift minivan into reverse in a parking garage in Luxembourg! We drove antique Fiats on a tour around Florence. We really made the most of the opportunity.

I also think travel is crucial for raising strong, confident kids. From the time my girls were teenagers, we had started taking them on trips to Europe, including both cruises and home exchanges, anything to get them in a new and challenging environment. When you travel, you run into unfamiliar situations, delays, and moments when you aren't sure where to go or what to do. Each time this would happen, I would point out to the girls, "Did you notice that I didn't have a magic solution to work through that issue because I'm mom? I just read the signs, asked for help, and solved the problem. There's no magic. You can do this, too." This helped build up their confidence muscles, and they both have been traveling independently, even to Europe with groups of students they didn't know, since they were teenagers. Nothing builds confidence better than facing a challenge and successfully navigating it.

Every trip I have taken with the girls has been special to me. But this time, when I returned home from the trip, refreshed and free, I had another new opportunity waiting. I had a whole new life as a single person. Footloose and fancy-free!

CHAPTER 8

RESTART #4: MEETING WES

Shortly before the trip, I had signed up on the dating site Match. com—thinking I might as well get started, since it would most likely take a few years for me to find someone I would really be interested in. Famous last words!

I couldn't believe how many nice, handsome, interesting, eligible men were on the site—in an appropriate age range for me and everything! I didn't expect anything serious to transpire anytime soon, but I thought: wouldn't it be nice just to have dinner with someone, or go to a movie with someone, who was actually interested in *me?*

I'm an old-fashioned girl and would never ask a man out "in the real world," but I feel like it's more acceptable online to at least make a friendly introduction. Let's face it: I lived in a very small town, not that close to the big city, so my profile might not get caught in anyone's net. And let's be real: men my age are often looking for someone at least five years younger. They can't help it; they just don't know any better! So I knew I needed to take it upon myself to reach out to a few interesting candidates just to catch their eye, nothing fancy.

I chose a one-hundred-mile radius and picked out some nice-looking men whose profiles seemed normal. I was pleasantly surprised to get good responses from three in particular whom I found interesting. Of course, I forget who the other two were now, but one of them turned out to be Wes...the love of my life. Since then, I have often joked that online dating is awesome. It's like shopping on Amazon. I just put Wes in my shopping cart and hit one-click checkout!

You have to understand that Wes was, and is, a handsome guy. Very handsome. So I was thrilled and a little surprised when I received a lengthy, well-thought-out response from him.

I was with my daughter Sealy and her friend in Houston at the Miss Texas pageant. Sealy was in the throes of competing for Miss Teen Texas. This was a good networking event for her, as well as a look ahead to her future—or so we thought. (But that is, yet again, another story.) After I received the response from Wes, I showed Sealy his profile. She said, "Yeah, he's out of your league." Of course I was just "mom" to her, so it didn't seem possible this guy would be interested in me. Not sure I was convinced, either.

I responded back and didn't hear anything for maybe twenty-four hours. Keep in mind, there were two other good prospects communicating regularly with me at this point and starting to hint around at wanting my cell phone number to take this thing a little farther. I wrote Wes back and said something to the effect of, "No pressure, not trying to be pushy, but I am curious if you have a real interest or if I should respond to these other guys. You definitely have me intrigued with your great letter you sent. But for all I know, you're just being kind, and perhaps you send great responses to everyone. So, it would be great if you could let me know if you are actually interested in talking further. If not, I wish you the best of luck either way."

And I ended by giving him my cell number. I really didn't want to give it to the other guys if Wes had a real interest.

Boy, did I get a response back quickly! I still remember the first line he texted: "Meet Wes Pack." Before that I only had his first name via the dating site.

We texted back and forth throughout the pageant weekend. I told him where we were and what we were doing. He said he didn't want to interrupt our time in Houston. I responded, "Hey, my kid isn't on stage right now, so we are all good!"

After several rounds of engaging banter via text, we could both see there was some potential chemistry. So, then he made his move. He asked if he could call me later that evening. I agreed but was *super* nervous. I hadn't done anything like this in nearly twenty years! As the time approached, the girls tried to convince me to talk to him while still in the hotel room with them! I said *no way* and found a spot out in the hall where I could sit down and talk. It was a little hard to hear, but we had instant chemistry. We laughed and told stories. We must have talked for an hour. It felt just easy and natural—so very normal for a situation that was so *not* normal for me.

He lived in Georgetown, just outside of Austin, and from that day on there was not a single day we didn't speak by phone and text. I was really looking forward to meeting him. Of course, we lived a hundred miles apart. I still look back and am so grateful I raised my distance parameter up to one hundred miles, because I just barely snagged him in my search at that distance!

Our phone calls quickly grew from one to two hours per night. We had such great rapport. And the one thing I loved about Wes from day one was that he was brutally open and honest.

BRUTAL HONESTY BUILDS INSTANT TRUST—AND THAT MEANS BEING HONEST WITH YOURSELF, TOO

Wes and I have both agreed that by the time you're our age and have lived a minute, you know what you're looking for. You also know what you don't want.

First of all, one benefit to a restart when you are a little older is that you're no longer looking for perfection because you know it doesn't exist. You know there will be hard times. There will be days when things aren't great, but if you find someone who is truly committed to the relationship, you can work past the choppy waters that are sure to come in this life.

People always ask me, "How did you find Wes?" And I tell them, "I think I wrote a great profile on Match.com where I was very honest. I knew it would attract the kind of person I'm interested in, and the person I'm not interested in wouldn't like it. And that's great. They can keep moving."

I literally said things in there like, "If you've never watched *Sein-*

feld and if you don't know the words to every Steve Miller band song, we're probably not going to be a fit."

I also used humor. I said, "Everybody on here says they're looking for a woman who's athletic and has an active lifestyle. I'm pretty sure you don't care if I live on Cheetos and Coke, as long as I'm thin. Well, I'm thin enough. I'm not particularly sporty, but I'm up for trying new things and I'll *be* a sport."

So, for people who were looking for honesty, a sense of humor, and a decent person who wasn't looking to pull something over on them, I felt it would be refreshing.

Wes knew he also had to be specific, and he had actually gone so far as to make a spreadsheet to help! He got honest with himself and literally made a spreadsheet of traits he was looking for that were nonnegotiable. When he would meet somebody, he didn't let himself get pulled in too quickly. Once some of those nonnegotiables weren't matching up, he moved on. That really empowered him to say no to people who didn't match up with what he wanted in his life moving forward.

Part of the benefit of us being in our late forties when we met, and not in our twenties, was that we had already learned so much about ourselves and what we wanted for our lives.

It also helped us give each other some grace along the way. When you've been through some difficult times and painful situations, it makes you appreciate each other far more when you do find someone worth holding onto.

Wes defaulted to being *overly* honest. In our first conversations, he would tell me all these awful things he had experienced. And he owned all of them. He said, "Yeah, I was just getting my butt kicked because I deserved it. I had it all coming." He was just in a place in his life where he was willing to have no delusions and to just be completely honest.

He would also tell me stories about high school, and he would talk about this friend or that friend. So when I looked him up on Facebook, I could see people with those same names commenting on his posts. They were still in his life. I said to myself, "Okay, here's someone who has a consistency to him. Those same people he tells those funny stories about are still present in his life. And it's all real. And they've maintained their relationships and their friendships." That was a very good sign. Not of a guy who is perfect, but a guy who is who and what he says he is. That was good enough for me.

That's where a whole lot of our base was formed. I trusted him from the beginning because he would just admit things he had done or situations in his life that he did not have to admit in our first few calls. But he did.

In fact, he went out of his way *not* to try to impress me with anything at all. He took responsibility for what *he* had done wrong in his previous two marriages. Then, he told me the story of how he had walked out of his last marriage with nothing at all and had started rebuilding his life. He took a job with a home building company, starting at the bottom. He would be the first one at work each day, sweeping out the model homes and doing all the tasks no one else wanted to do. By the time we met he had worked his way up to the head salesman in the branch. He knew he would advance if he could just get his foot in the door. He could have just told me about his impressive current position. He didn't have to tell me where he started, just a year before. But the fact that he was willing to share that went a long way in helping me trust him. Most people don't get that. They think sharing their struggles makes them look weak, but it doesn't. It makes them look honest and builds immediate trust.

I find that our human instinct to impress is completely the opposite of what works. I'm pretty sure I'm not the only one who is most impressed by those not trying to impress. If you are willing to say, "I didn't know that," or "I messed that up; let me see how I can fix it," I have *far* more interest in what you have to say in general. I think we all struggle with this. We often see not knowing something as a weakness. No one knows everything! The person who is pretending they do is basically lying—to themselves and to others. And, unbeknownst to them, they are losing the respect of everyone all along the way.

A NEW HAPPILY EVER AFTER

After Wes and I began dating, we seemed to be a source of great interest and curiosity to people. After all, I was newly divorced after eighteen years of marriage and living in a small town! What more do you need to get the gossip wheel churning?

One of the first times Wes came to town to visit, we were walking down our town's charming Main Street, heading to lunch. At that time, I still had the retail store downtown, so of course after lunch we stopped in to say hello to the ladies working. They were laughing and said they had a great story for me. The owner of the store next door had seen us walking down the street and quickly popped in to ask them, "Who is that handsome man Tammy is parading up and down the street?"

Here I thought we were just going to lunch. Turns out we were parading, which is apparently a verb in Texas!

I can't tell you how many people came up to me while Wes and I were dating and said, "I've never seen you look so happy! You're always smiling!"

For some reason, people just seemed to be interested in the story of Wes and me. They were intrigued by the transformation, at age forty-seven, of someone they had always known in the local business community—someone who was very serious and dependable. Suddenly, I was the person with the biggest smile in the world—and, at least relative to my past, I was in the most glamorous new relationship. I think the fact that Wes is not only handsome, but that his face and aura just exude genuineness, was also part of the appeal.

I went in to visit with a local builder shortly before I met Wes, to look into options for adding B&B cottages behind an inn I owned. This gentleman and I had known each other in a superficial way for many years, like saying hi at the local gas station pit stop each morning when I stopped in for my Diet Coke. So, to get it out of the way, I told him, "You have probably heard that I'm getting divorced..."

He immediately said, "I never knew you were married!"

What a sobering thought! It made me realize how shallow a relationship I'd had with my ex-husband. Someone who had been in the same small town for all eighteen years of my marriage, with both of us actively involved in Chamber of Commerce activities, charities, and more, had never even seen me with my ex-husband.

When I speak on using social media to build your business, I always tell people they need to focus on their story. They often look at me like, "What on earth is my story?" What I learned in all of this is that *other people* will tell you what your story is. They told me. Not on purpose, but by constantly reinforcing how happy they were to see me so happy, to see that smile on my face. Without telling me, they were telling me. They weren't telling me how excited they were about that new window display I was working on at the retail store. They were relating to, and interested in, the transformation of a life at age forty-seven, at a time when you might think your life path was set. Were they thinking that they, too, might have it in them to make a happiness restart? I bet some of them were. At least, I hope so.

It took only a few months for Wes and me to realize that what we had was the real thing. I knew this was the man I wanted to build my new life with. Our physical attraction for each other was powerful, but so was our genuine "like" of one another. Wes's outlook on life was refreshing, with a completely unjaded and youthful enthusiasm! He was always smiling and just so positive. So, once we decided this was *it*, we started to plan the wedding.

A big wedding was out of the question, as I felt it would be in bad taste. But a small, local wedding ran too high a risk of offending everyone not invited. When you've lived in a town for twenty years, it's hard to have a small wedding!

We decided that a destination wedding made sense for us! It would just be us and our five kids. But when you can go anywhere in the world, how do you choose? I'll tell you how *I* chose. When the wedding is over, you have the memories, and you have the photographs. So, I looked for the best photographer I could find. I came across the most fabulous couple: One and Only Paris Photographers, in Paris, France. We chose that as our location, and I had a great time planning the wedding over the coming months. The photos were incredible, and I shared them on Facebook, of course. I really credit the story of our falling in love, culminating in that beautiful wedding, for creating a following that we then used to build a new business together. Attention is one of the most powerful currencies in existence today. It's one of the few that you can acquire just by being willing to put yourself out there and tell *your* story.

REVERSE AGING

I look back at my photos from my forties and even my thirties and, for various reasons, I actually look better now, in my fifties. From around the time I married Wes, people have been telling me they hardly recognize me and that I actually look younger and better than in the past. Let's face it: the way we look impacts the way we feel about ourselves and the way we act and treat others. It is far more important than *only* what we see in the mirror.

I attribute this major renewal to a few factors. First, my appearance actually mattered again. In my eighteen-year marriage, there were phases where I was simply focusing on work and the kids and not putting much effort into my appearance. Then, there were times when I dieted, exercised, wore cute clothes, and really fixed myself up. The result was the same; he still just wasn't interested in me either way.

I remember one time in particular, we went to the local Hospital Gala. I was in great shape, bought a beautiful gown, and looked, if I do say so, about as good as I ever had. We had a very nice evening, and I received many compliments, which I thought would have made him proud. Then we got back home, and he remarked what a fun evening it had been, said goodnight, and headed upstairs to *his bedroom*. I remember crying myself to sleep, thinking, *What is wrong with me?* Honestly, even that night, I would stop myself and say, "No, what is wrong with *him?*"

Once he moved out of the house in 2013, I finally started focusing on *me*. I was still working in my businesses but had quite a bit of free time. I went to market a couple times a year for the retail stores, came to staff meetings, and did some display work, but I had more time on my hands than I'd had in a while. So I started to focus on my diet, and I started seeing a personal trainer five mornings a week. I began lifting weights and doing cardio, and I started feeling great! By the time the divorce was finalized, and I was ready to look at online dating sites, I was looking pretty good.

I also discovered the Real Housewife series around this time. Don't laugh. I know those women can act crazy sometimes— okay, most times—but I realized that most of them were in my age range, and they looked *amazing*. I knew they put a lot of effort into their appearance, and I didn't have to go as far as they did to just do a little freshen-up. So I had Botox (which I had done maybe twice before then, sporadically). I had fillers in my cheekbones to get the shape of my face back—aging tends to hollow out the face, and fillers can reverse that effect. I had a tummy tuck in 2017, not for weight loss but to get rid of the sag from two C-sections. Later, I got porcelain veneers for my teeth to correct an overlap of my front two teeth that was beginning to worsen. Bottom line is I started to invest some time, money, and energy into *myself*.

One thing I am *not* saying is that you should or should not do any of these things. If you are happy and comfortable in your skin, then that's fantastic. If, however, you think negatively more than once a day about your weight or appearance, you should do something about it! Empower yourself to make the change. It doesn't have to be extreme, just something that makes you feel better about yourself—more like you are living your best life, not just existing, and not waiting around to die. Not projecting all your thoughts, hopes, and dreams on your children and their appearance, but on yourself!

I see so many mothers living vicariously through how thin, attractive, or popular their daughters are, while completely giving up on their own appearance. Your children are not you. You are you, and you are responsible for taking care of yourself. We live in the most amazing time where these things are actually possible and within the reach of most of us. If you need to take steps to be healthier and look and feel better, do it!

I would say one of my most popular social media posts I've ever made, and certainly the one that got the most ongoing feedback, was my "before and after" post. People still mention that post to me at conferences when they see me. The interesting thing is that I was maybe ten or fifteen pounds lighter *at most* in the after pictures—so it's not like I lost a hundred pounds. It's just that I slowly but surely worked on improving *everything* about myself.

And, trust me, the journey never ends. As I type this, I am continuing to work on healthier eating. There is no single magic bullet that fixes our health-and-appearance situation permanently. It's a natural battle that never ends. The important thing is never giving up!

After all, I'd once again need to be in great shape, physically and mentally—because another restart was coming.

CHAPTER 9

RESTART #5: ANOTHER CAREER SHIFT

Wes and I married in March of 2015. He had worked his way up to a great position with the home building company in George-town, and I didn't want to be that pushy partner who insisted he give up his world and move to be with me. I knew I had to come up with an *amazing* option for him to want to leave that opportunity in Georgetown and move to Fredericksburg. Georgetown is a nice town just outside of Austin, but my girls were still in school in Fredericksburg. Plus, my businesses were there.

Wes was working in new home sales at the time. That type of sales position doesn't require a real estate license, but he had already taken the real estate course, just not the exam. I told him that real estate was the one business I had been turn-ing away for years. I already had the retail stores—two, at that time—as well as my own B&Bs and the B&B service. On my own,

I simply could not add real estate (other than to do my own deals). But with Wes on board, we could really build something in the real estate world.

We spent the rest of 2015 creating our own brokerage. We found a sponsoring broker company, created our LLC, and started putting together our company. When deciding what to call it, we knew we would be new on the scene but didn't want to be seen as "new" to town. Absolute Charm had been the name of my first B&B cottage in 2001 and was also the name of our new reservation service, which had been around since 2007. So it didn't take much effort to settle on Absolute Charm Real Estate as our name.

People often ask where we came up with the name Absolute Charm. The reservation service we used in the beginning recommended something early in the alphabet so people would view our cottage first. So I said out loud, "Well a, aa...no. Ab. Absolute. Absolute something. Absolute Charm?"

They liked it, and I liked it, and that was it. That one little cottage we renovated on the side of our house back in 2000, thinking it would be a guesthouse for grandma, was officially named Absolute Charm in under sixty seconds—and that name is still with us all these years later.

We then sorted out our colors, fonts, and sign design, and a new real estate company was born! It was just Wes and me at first, and we had an impressive three total sales in 2015, the first being in November. Truth be told, two of the three sales were us buying and selling places for ourselves!

MORE TOOLS IN THE TOOLBOX

The beauty of restarting as you get older is you are no longer starting with a shiny new toolbox. No, by now, you have earned some tools in your toolbox. The edges are a little dinged up and rusty. Life has left a mark, but that toolbox is far more capable of helping you to get through than when it was new and shiny and still had its price tag stuck on the bottom.

Wes and I knew we were not starting off wet behind the ears. We were both good at marketing and having good ideas, and we both knew how to sell. So, we took those skills we earned the hard way—with blood, sweat, and tears—from our toolbox and said, "This time, we're restarting a little older, but with far more tools."

We knew that with both of us working together, we could be really good in our new chosen field, and we could be really good really fast.

We researched the quality of the brokerages in our town, and we saw that there was a gap in the level of marketing for the modern age. We believed we could do better.

Because we were starting later in life, we knew we had to go at it aggressively, be smart, be on social media, marketing, marketing, marketing, because we wanted to be number one sooner than later.

I didn't know much about real estate at the time, in terms of as a business, other than that it's very cyclical. But I was pretty sure the guys at the top didn't drop to zero sales just because the market got softer. The brokerage that was seventeenth in the market was probably hurting under those conditions, but I was sure that numbers one, two, and three were just fine. That meant we had to make sure that by the time the cycle came back around, we were number one—or at least number two or three.

So we used the tools we'd built over all those years and worked together. We took each of our experiences, shared our opinions and vision with each other, compromised where we needed to, and made it work.

MAKING IT WORK

We really believed in going big from day one, so we started an all-out marketing blitz with color ads in the local paper, post-cards—you name it. We were new in real estate, but we had a *lot* of life and business experience, so that is what we focused on.

We also started using social media to leverage all that we did. One listing could look like three or four when photographed from different angles and at different times of day, both inside and outside.

My social media strategy just kind of evolved naturally as a result of what was happening. I realized we could magnify all our efforts for our clients by posting on social media. And to make sure the maximum number of people saw the posts, I needed the maximum number of Facebook friends. Facebook allows you to have five thousand friends, so why would I ever want fewer than that? That would be like being offered five thousand glossy magazines all about yourself, your listings, and your events that would be mailed out for free by a generous benefactor—but telling them, "No, just mail out 1,317 copies for me, please." No one would do that! Having 1,317 Facebook friends is equally wasteful. Use those spots. Fill them with people who might do business with you someday—people with whom you can have a mutually beneficial relationship of some kind.

I realized how well this social media strategy works when we hadn't had a *single* closing yet but a realtor friend at church came up to us and said, "Man, y'all are *killing* it!" So of course I said, "*Yeah,* we are!" Perception is reality. It just is.

Then my friend and B&B service manager Tami Smith and another reservation agent, Emaly, who also worked at our reservation service, got their real estate licenses. Around the same time, we were fortunate enough to bring on a very experienced agent, Catherine, from another brokerage. She really kept us in line doing things correctly in those early years. I always say she kept us out of real estate jail! We knew how to market and how to sell, but it was *extremely* valuable having someone who knew what to put in all those blanks!

Over the coming years, we added agents and grew the team to a nice, comfortable size of sixteen, as of this writing. In under three years, we became the number one office in town! That same year, 2018, we joined eXp Realty on the brokerage side and converted into a team.

We knew we were starting this business later in life and wanted to be number one sooner than later, so we poured a ton of heart and soul *and money* into it. When I ran the numbers while writing this book, I found that our real estate team has done $70 million in sales, whereas the number two team has done about

$40 million in sales, and number three has done $20-something million. Going all-in really paid off for us!

We consider ourselves so fortunate to have maintained that top-level sales volume for several years now. We have an established brand and a team we dearly love. (There are so many strategies for going from zero to number one in under three years that I am eager to share with you all, but that will definitely need to be another book!)

WORKING ON *US*, TOO

Wes and I are constantly evolving too. We're trying to be conscious on an ongoing basis to improve ourselves and our lives.

We recently bought a second home in Natchez, Mississippi, which has been another restart for us. Fredericksburg is our primary home, and most likely always will be, but it has been so enjoyable to go to this other town that is like its own world. It is such a different culture than the one we have in Fredericksburg. Natchez is more social than, well, anywhere else on earth! We have already made so many wonderful friends there, so we get lots of invites to do fun things. Recently, we were asked to join friends there for three different outings within the same twenty-four-hour period; that's what we would do in an entire *year* in Fredericksburg!

We think of our second home as a restart because it shows that it's not too late to become part of another town, another set of friends—another whole world—and it has been a real joy to experience that.

CHAPTER 10

═══

SAVANNAH'S RESTART

When my oldest daughter Savannah was around twelve years old, she was in the height of her dance class days. During each competition season, she typically had two solos, one or two duos and trios, and three or more group dances. She spent over ten hours per week at the studio—and I spent a good bit of time there, as well, visiting with the other moms. I wasn't much of a soccer mom, as my girls weren't very interested in the sport, but I was definitely a dance mom.

One day, as I was picking Savannah up from dance practice, my friend told me that neither of our girls had been selected for a special advanced jazz group the studio was starting. Then she mentioned that Sarah, a girl who typically had not been a very strong dancer, had made the group. I knew this was the type of thing that could really be upsetting to a girl Savannah's age in that oh-so-sensitive time of life.

After Savannah climbed into the back seat, I asked about her day and then said, "Hey, I heard y'all didn't get into the special jazz group but Sarah did."

She nodded.

"Well, how did that happen?" I asked.

She replied flatly, "She was better than us."

I was a bit incredulous. "But she's never been very good."

"Well, she was good today! She must have been practicing. Her arabesques were beautiful!"

I immediately felt my disappointment turning to pride because in that moment, for the first time, this characteristic of self-awareness came racing onto my radar. Being a typical mom, I thought I needed to say something encouraging, so I threw in for good measure, "But you'll always be one of the best tap dancers."

Savannah kind of shrugged and said, "Yeah, I know," as if to say *what does one thing have to do with the other?*

I wasn't happy that she didn't make it into the advanced group, but I was *ecstatic* that she could step outside of herself and view the situation so objectively, without feeling bad about herself.

This scenario was repeated a few years later when Savannah was a freshman at Pepperdine University working on an engineering degree. She was always really good at math, but to study engineering, she had to take a lot of physics classes. She did not have a strong science background, and physics was turning out to be a huge challenge. She took part in all the study sessions put together by her classmates and even found a tutor an hour away, a UCLA PhD candidate. I have taken some pretty hard classes in my life, but never one where I literally couldn't understand what was being said. Apparently, that's not an uncommon feeling in physics classes!

While preparing for a major exam, Savannah called and said she added up the time she had spent that week just on that one physics class: a whopping thirty hours! That sounded overwhelming to me since she was also taking four other classes.

She took the test and called me to report that she made a fifty-two.

"Oh no; I'm sorry," I said.

"Oh, it's okay; that was around the class average, so with the curve, it's a B!"

I can't imagine a class where a fifty-two is the middle score! I couldn't help but question her once more: "But you spent thirty hours preparing for the test. Maybe this isn't for you?"

Without skipping a beat, she responded, "I'll just have to work harder."

At that moment, I knew one thing for sure: she would succeed in anything she did, and I told her so. I knew for certain she had internalized that rarest of qualities: extreme self-awareness.

SELF-AWARENESS

Most of us in Savannah's situation would likely have blamed the test, the teacher, or pretty much anything else we could find to blame, especially after studying so hard for so long. The fact that she understood at an early age that the buck stopped with her was what would propel her to success in *any* undertaking.

Self-awareness has become a bit of a buzzword in recent years, but it is something I have thought about for a long time. To me, the concept of self-awareness is very straightforward: it is simply the ability to view yourself objectively, to fully understand your strengths and weaknesses without attaching judgment to the result.

One of the main benefits of having high self-awareness is that it creates trust in those around you. For example, Wes was so honest when we first met, so open about talking about the things he had done well in life along with the mistakes he had made. Probably without realizing it, he was making it easy for me to trust him. If he had only talked about his abilities and things he did well, I would have instinctively been waiting to find his flaws for myself. Because, let's face it: we all know that no one is perfect.

My younger daughter Sealy spent two years at Berklee College of Music in Boston. She would call me after a test, an audition, or a performance to fill me in on how she did. Over time, I realized I could be completely confident when she told me she had done well, because she would also be the first to call me when she *hadn't* done well and say, "Boy, that was embarrassing... I was awful!"

But let's talk for a moment about those who *lack* self-awareness. I believe they come in three flavors: those who are overly dismissive of their abilities; those who erroneously believe they can do it all; and those who are confident but a little confused about what they are actually good at.

FALSE MODESTY

People who are overly dismissive of their abilities are perhaps the most difficult to be around. Everyone is good at something, but this group has such an extreme lack of self-esteem (and self-awareness!) that they are ready to give up at a moment's notice.

As I mentioned earlier, I remember Sealy coming home from elementary school and saying that her pet peeve was one of the girls in her class who was reasonably good at art but would always say her project wasn't any good. Even at that age, it was obvious to Sealy that the girl was simply showing false modesty to get attention. "She just wants everyone to brag on how good her drawing is," she would say. Modesty is a virtue; false modesty is not.

If you tend to put down yourself and your abilities, stop it. Start to listen to yourself, and when you start using false modesty, take note and change your stance. Embracing your gifts and abilities does *not* equate to claiming that you are perfect. It does *not* set you up for failure in the event you don't perfectly execute in one of the areas of talent. I believe some people feel if they set the bar low enough, anything positive they achieve is going to be amplified.

Wes is an extremely talented, natural artist. He just sees things differently and interprets them beautifully. Whenever the topic would come up, you could see him squirm a bit when I told people what a great artist he is. He would often say, "Michelangelo is an artist; I'm a hack." As soon as we were alone, I admonished him, "Don't you *ever* call yourself a hack again. You are loaded with God-given talent, so stop denying it!"

The goal of self-awareness is to find an honest balance where you embrace your talents and acknowledge the areas where you need to improve.

"I CAN DO EVERYTHING"

The second group of people who are lacking in self-awareness have great self-esteem but think they can do it all. Of course, this can lead to exceeding your area of competence and underserving people you have made promises to.

No one, absolutely *no one,* is good at everything. I have had a few agents in the past sit around our conference table during training and just nod and agree with everything—no matter what the training topic was—as if to say, "Yep, I already knew that!" They had already done that. Nothing new to them! Every once in a while, it's nice to say, "That's interesting; I didn't realize that." Putting off an air of being a know-it-all is usually a clue to others that you don't know much at all! Showing others that you are always willing to listen, to learn, and to improve is far more appealing than putting on a false show that nothing's news to you.

WHAT ARE YOU GOOD AT?

The third group is also confident but tends to confuse what they *enjoy* doing with what they are *good* at. Who wouldn't prefer doing what they enjoy? But enjoying a task doesn't make you good at it; so you have to take an honest assessment of likes vs. abilities.

I've known people in church, for example, who really enjoyed leading the congregational singing, but they weren't very good at it. Make sure you are actually talented enough to do a job well, rather than simply enjoying it yourself, before you subject others to your muscle-flexing.

It's okay to need outside affirmation of what your best skills are. It's always okay to be genuinely vulnerable and open to feedback. But often, this group decides that they are good at something when they absolutely are not. Everyone is good at something, but being confused about your innate gifts can be detrimental and frustrating. My best suggestion in this situation is to ask those who know you best to share what your talents are and—if you are strong enough to handle the truth—where you still need to improve.

We all fall somewhere on the self-awareness spectrum. Some of the most self-aware people I know are my two daughters. This doesn't mean they're good at everything; it just means they are realistic about where they shine and where they don't. I attribute this somewhat to their DNA. *No one* can be descended from my mother and be oblivious in this area. But it's also due to their upbringing. In our household we had a very low tolerance for excuses *or* exaggeration.

MAKING A TOUGH DECISION

Within a year, despite working hard to maintain A's and B's in her classes, Savannah and I both came to the conclusion that she should quit college and move home to join us in our newest business, our real estate brokerage. She was doing well in all of her classes, but it was obvious her heart wasn't in it.

I was the kind of kid who loved studying nearly anything—learning about Chinese architecture sounds fascinating to me; to Savannah, it does not. Instead, she developed her entrepreneurial chops *much* younger than I did. Again, I attribute this to a combination of nature and nurture.

Savannah was really interested in real estate, so while she was in college she had an unpaid internship one afternoon a week where she worked with an up-and-coming agent in California, helping him with whatever he needed. She was just naturally drawn to the field.

She would call me in the mornings while walking to class and give me ideas of contests we should do with the team to get the agents excited about prospecting. She is also a natural networker, great at making strategic connections and knowing when to leverage them and when to hold back.

On one hand, she was in an enviable position of having parents who were willing and able to pay for her education. On the other hand, she knew she had four more years of her five-year-degree plan where she could either be starting her career or finishing her degree—a degree she would never use. It was clearer by the day that she would never work as an engineer, shut off in a cubicle, alone. I asked her, "Is it important to you to have the degree, because of what other people think? We'll support you either way, but it has to be *your* choice."

So, she made the *very* difficult decision to quit school and come home. At the tender age of nineteen, Savannah was making *her* first restart!

She teared up as the decision was made. She wasn't sad to leave school; she was sad to say goodbye to one vision of her future. She dreaded telling her friends and cohorts because of the social stigma associated with making this choice. She knew there would be those who would pity her and some who would even spread rumors that she flunked out of college, which couldn't be further from the truth.

When she began telling people, they all said the same thing: "You can always go back." Savannah said from the moment the decision was made, she knew she would never go back. In her heart, she knew it was the right decision for *her*, and she was learning the same lesson I had learned in moot court, in law school: to listen to and trust her own voice.

In my eyes, Savannah is a hero because she accepted what she knew was right for her, *and* she was willing to stand up against the narrow-minded belief that college is the only pathway to success.

Unfortunately, our society has decided there is only one acceptable path to success: going to college and then finding a "real" job. To find real success by following a different path, however, you have to be self-aware and mentally strong enough to swim against the current of popular belief.

I may be the perfect person to argue that college is not right for everyone. I clearly don't have an axe to grind against education, since I have a law degree. But this country needs to wake up and realize there is no one-size-fits-all solution. If you want to be a doctor, a nurse, a pharmacist, a teacher, and many other jobs, you absolutely have to have a degree. If you are going to be an entrepreneur, however, you may be giving up valuable time when you could have been building connections and honing your practical skills. Self-awareness will be the most important skill you need to have to be able to make the right decision for yourself.

SAVANNAH HITS HER STRIDE

Right before she quit school, I took Savannah with me to California for a whirlwind four-hour real estate marketing mastermind with a very elite group. We flew to California and back in one day. At the end of that day, I shared with her that the information gained in those four hours would equal all the practical knowledge she could hope to gain in a full semester at college. She agreed.

In May of 2020, Savannah would have been scheduled to graduate college. I am happy to say that for the past three years, she has been in the top twenty-five agents in our local MLS, which is unbelievable for someone her age. In 2019, at the age of twenty-two, she sold over $6 million, and she doubled that in 2020, selling over $12 million and landing in the top ten agents in our town. In 2021, she ranked even higher.

She also took her first real estate commissions and put a down payment on a van to start her wine tour business and hired her first driver—her dad. Their relationship has come full circle and been a great blessing to both of them. She is currently preparing to roll out her third tour vehicle, is renovating a vacation rental that she purchased 50/50 with her dad, is working full time in real estate, and has recently married a great guy who supports her in all she does. And she is twenty-five years old—with many restarts in her future, but already with a strong foundation to support her through whatever comes next.

Like most of us, Savannah is excellent at some things and terrible at others. She's very logical and cuts to the point as fast as anyone I know. I always say if I am hit by a bus and no longer here, Savannah knows exactly what I would do in every situation. She struggles mightily, however, with spelling and grammar. She misspells the simplest words. But here is the thing: that wasn't improving despite years of education. As she would say, "I can pay someone to help me with that."

And she's right. We all have strengths and weaknesses, but it is only when we are *aware* of what those strengths and weaknesses are that we can begin to address them—to use our strengths to our advantage and learn how to overcome our weaknesses.

EVERYBODY HAS THEIR OWN STRUGGLES AND SUCCESSES

Recently, our whole family went to a wedding—Wes, me, all our kids, and even my daughters' father. In the car on the way home, our youngest son, Bridger, said, "I just don't know how I'm ever going to be able to afford a home."

I told him, "You're twenty-four years old! You keep comparing yourself to me and your dad now, but we had jack-squat when we were twenty-four. Besides, you're at school, and you're working hard. You're in a good place on your own path."

Then he said, "Well, it's hard not to make comparisons when you have a super-star sister like Savannah."

I'll tell you what I told him: Savannah has entrepreneurial chops like nobody you'll ever meet. Without a doubt, she's done some amazing things. But people—even her brother—don't always see the other side. For example, yes, she and her dad have gone fifty-fifty on a B&B project, but you don't see that the renovation has taken two years, during which time they've each paid $2,500 a month with nobody staying there and no money coming in. Why *would* they go around telling people about that? All anyone can see is that she is crushing it—and she is—but she also got kicked in the tail with a larger-than-expected tax bill, despite being on top of all her estimates. I could go through every one of her successes and still talk about all the times where Savannah said she couldn't sleep at night because of the stress.

We tend to see only the glamour and the wins, because that is what people show on the outside. But every single person, even that one you think has it all together, has some struggles and failures to go along with their success. Those struggles are typically private and not something most people feel comfortable talking about with the broader world. But rest assured, the struggle is real. And it's universal.

One of my favorite expressions my mom used to say was, "Whether it's raising kids or having a business, if you're successful, *you're gonna know you did it*." You will have paid the price and cried in the shower and worried and stressed and had heart palpitations and everything else that goes with the amount of pressure that's on someone who's had that success.

It's similar to looking at people on social media and saying, "Oh, they have it all together. They have everything. Their life is perfect." But you don't know what's going on behind the scenes or what went on behind the scenes so they could get there. What built up to that? When people see the pictures I post, they don't know everything I've gone through, either.

What's important to remember is that you don't know most people's backstory, and they don't know yours. Your backstory is important—not so you can say, "Look how far I've come and how great I am," but so you can remember that wherever you are now, you can get to wherever you want to go.

There's no magic bullet here. I didn't pop out with the success I have at this moment. I started with a whole bunch of hard times I had to go through. So, if you're going through those hard times right now, know that you can go through them and get to the good. You just have to make the choice to keep going.

Like Mom said, when you get there, you're gonna know you did it.

I know I did it when it comes to raising my kids, because I ended up with two strong, amazing daughters. But it was never easy. And I don't foresee still waters and perfect smooth sailing in the future, either!

CHAPTER 11

===

SEALY STARTS OVER

My younger daughter, Sealy, has already created her own restart, too.

She finished her degree in 2020. For the first year and a half of the COVID-19 pandemic, she was a server in Fredericksburg. At the end of 2021, though, Sealy said, "I don't want to live in Texas anymore. I want to move somewhere else, and I think we're going to move to Raleigh-Durham, North Carolina, because house prices are really good there."

Savannah laughed and said, "What are you talking about? You're twenty-three—you're way too young to retire to the suburbs! You've never even been to Raleigh-Durham before. What are you going to do, get a bigger house so your cats have more room? You're Berklee College of Music educated; you love the arts; you've always loved the big city. For crying out loud, go live in Manhattan! Every opportunity is there. Do it for a year, two years, or the rest of your life. You pick, but just take your shot!"

(Did I tell you my girls are smart, or what?)

Well, Sealy listened to her big sister. In January of 2022, Sealy took her shot and moved to New York City with her girlfriend, Lucinda; and her restart is going really well.

NO GUARANTEES

Nothing is guaranteed in life, but what I really appreciated about Savannah's advice to Sealy is the reminder that nothing has to be permanent if you don't want it to be. You can make a big move, see what it's like for a year, and just try it. If you don't like it, you can move back. In Sealy's case, she could move back to Texas or to Raleigh-Durham, or somewhere else she hasn't even thought of yet.

But if you *don't* take that shot, you run the risk of being seventy years old and thinking, "I wish I had moved to Manhattan when I was younger."

I'm fifty-five, and I don't have a desire to live in Manhattan—but if someone had given me an opportunity like that back when I was in my twenties, it would have been so cool! That is the age to try different things, with the knowledge that you can make another change later. As Gary Vee says, when you're in your twenties and thirties, you're still a baby. You should be testing everything you could possibly want to do, taking every chance that might exist. Try on new opportunities and ideas; see what happens. Sometimes, that will open up yet another possibility that you can't even see yet from where you are now—that you might never see without shifting and opening up a bit.

You can still make changes and have restarts even after your twenties and thirties, but that is the time of life for exploration and discovery. You never know when saying yes to an opportunity could lead to something magical!

CHARCUTERIE AND SPREADSHEETS

When Sealy moved to Manhattan, we knew housing would be expensive, but also that she could make a lot as a server there. She had to take a test to become a server at her current restaurant in Manhattan. The owners told the potential servers, "If you don't score an eighty-five or better on this test, you will be demoted."

Sealy was so stressed out studying for the test at this high-end restaurant, but the day of the exam, she texted me, "I can't believe I was so worried. I got the highest score out of everybody!"

I wasn't surprised, because she always dedicates a lot of time to her work, puts all of herself into it, and really enjoys what she does. Even before she moved to Manhattan, she was a server at a really nice restaurant in Fredericksburg called Vaudeville. At this restaurant, when a customer orders a charcuterie board, the servers come up with the boards themselves. They go in the back and invent their own combinations and creations.

She learned that when she put certain combinations of ingredients together, the chef would walk by and say, for example, "Never put that cheese with that sauce."

So, she started making lists of what Chef said not to combine, and then she went a step further. During her downtime at home, she made a spreadsheet listing all the meats, cheeses, condiments, and other accompaniments. Then she put Xs next to the pairings the chef had warned her against and checkmarks next to the ones she knew worked.

But she didn't stop there. She asked the chef if he would tell her when he had half an hour to sit down with her and go over everything so she knew what worked and what didn't for every possible combination. Then she designed a chart so he didn't have to keep repeating to people not to put certain things together.

I said, "You went home, on your own time, and made this spreadsheet that can now be printed and posted there at the restaurant for every server. You created an actual defined process, which is every employer's dream." I know this because most business owners are more art-driven than process-driven. Show me a great entrepreneur, and I will bet you they are weak on process but strong on creation.

SEALY'S PHONE INTERVIEW

When Sealy moved to New York in January of 2022, it was a terrible time—another wave of coronavirus had just hit, and no one was hiring. She pounded the pavement, but found it difficult to find a job. Even though she had glowing references, every restaurant asked, "But do you have *New York* experience?"

She told me, "I learned pretty early on that I was going to have to go with a brand-new restaurant, because that's the only place that would hire someone who didn't have New York experience."

Finally, she got a phone interview with the managers of a new restaurant.

On the day of her call, she sent me a picture of her wearing her business suit, with the text, "I'm all ready for my interview!"

I texted back, "Oh, is it a video call?"

"No," she said, "it's just by phone. But I know that if I'm all dressed up, decked out, and professional, I'm going to interview better, even over the phone."

"Good luck!" I told her.

A little while later, I got one more text: "I finished my interview. Now I can take off all these business clothes!"

Again, I was so impressed. She knew that if she felt polished and professional on the outside, they would hear it in her voice. Her enthusiasm would come through, even in a phone interview. And, even though they couldn't see what shoes she was wearing, she was confident she had put her best foot forward. Of course she got the job.

ALWAYS EXCEED EXPECTATIONS

Sealy is a good example of the idea that opportunities appear to people who exceed expectations. She knows where she is weaker, and we *all* have weaknesses. In the areas where she is strong, she over-delivers. She has realized one of her weaknesses is not being naturally "warm" like one of the other servers is. Sealy's strength is knowing the menu and being more prepared than the other servers. She says, "I'm the 'smart one,' so I can't let my menu pop-quiz scores slip. I've got to double down on what I'm already good at."

Remember, focus on what you can control. You control what you do. You control *how much* you do. Therefore, you can control whether you are simply meeting or exceeding expectations. You can't always control what opportunities come your way, but you can control how much effort you put into those opportunities.

Others will always notice you and reward you in various ways for exceeding expectations. How do you know they will notice? Because so few people actually exceed expectations—at least not on a consistent basis. If you hear comments such as "always goes above and beyond" or "always goes the extra mile" from coworkers, supervisors, and friends, you are on the right track.

If, on the other hand, you *fail* to exceed expectations, you fall into the large mass of mediocrity: a slow-moving cesspool of humanity unwilling to do more, to be better. That's not a place I want to be! To live an extraordinary life, you have to *be* extra ordinary! If you want to live a life of success and fulfillment, do the work to develop the skills, the work ethic, and the grit required to get there.

What can you do to exceed expectations? If you think about it, you already know the answer. Get there earlier. Stay later. Do the job no one wants to do. Never look for credit. If you don't look for credit (and you will need to check your deepest motivations here to keep them in check), then credit will always find you. People can sense those doing the right thing and the tough thing to receive praise. And they can also sense those who are doing it because, like most skills, it either comes naturally or you have worked hard to create that "muscle memory" of behavior. Either way, the result is the same. You earn respect—not only from others, but also from yourself.

I DON'T HAVE TO OUTRUN THE BEAR; I ONLY HAVE TO OUTRUN *YOU*

You've probably heard the story where a hunter asks another hunter what they should do if they see a bear. The first hunter says, "You should run." The second hunter asks, "How can you think you can possibly outrun a bear?" The first hunter replies, "I don't have to outrun the bear; I only have to outrun you."

I was reminded of this story recently when Sealy started working at the first restaurant willing to give a chance to someone with "no New York experience." She immediately realized this restaurant was very corporate and wanted to project that image. So, every day, she showed up in a suit and made sure to give off the professional feeling they wanted.

She and another person—let's call him Marvin—were hired to be "founding servers," since they were the first servers hired for the restaurant's grand opening.

Marvin showed up right on time every day and always did a good job. So, Sealy started showing up ten minutes early. By the time Marvin arrived, she had already written out the tasks for the day so she could just hand him a list of things to do.

"That's great," I told her when I heard about her position. "You really want to be the head of the pack."

"Yeah," she said, "but in reality, all I have to do is be better than Marvin!"

By just doing the smallest things—she wasn't showing up an hour early, just ten minutes—she'd already outperformed him.

And those little things set her apart. By the time the restaurant officially opened, they had promoted her to supervisor and given her a raise.

Again, people who exceed expectations find new opportunities where others can't even see them. When young people come to me and say they're worried about finding the next opportunity, I tell them not to worry about that. Instead, focus on exceeding expectations. It's a better use of your energy.

ANOTHER RESTART FOR SEALY!

Since I first wrote this section, Sealy has had another restart already! She attacked working at the new restaurant with all the fervor she usually does. We all were sure she would work hard and do well, and that her tip income would be excellent (we all know how expensive New York restaurants are). But, as is often the case, there was a fly in the ointment. What we did not know is that nearly all restaurants in New York City use a "tip pool" method where everyone's tips for the day go into the pool and come out based on a percentage. For example, those in the bar each receive 5 percent of the pool, all servers receive 4 percent, and so on.

In Texas, she was accustomed to "tipping out" a small percentage of her tips to go to the support staff, but she kept over 90 percent of what she herself had earned. In New York, her tips were averaging $500 to $1,000 per day, sometimes more, but this was an average day for her. After putting it all into the tip pool, she was walking away with just over $200 each day, the same as other servers who were *not* pushing the $200 tomahawk steak or the upgraded bottle of wine. This did not go over well.

I assured her that there would probably be a backlash from the staff and they would likely unite and request a change in the system. This is when she helped *me* realize there were two kinds of people in her restaurant, and everywhere in the world. First, there were those who liked the system because there was so much support staff they didn't have to work very hard. Then there was her. Apparently, she was the only one who would prefer to work much harder, with little support, and keep the majority of what she earned.

She began to be disenchanted with not only the pay system but the environment in general. After giving it a lot of thought, she came to the conclusion that even if the pay system were adjusted, she wasn't sure she could make a career out of working alongside people who were so complacent. While she enjoyed the company of many of her coworkers, she realized she wanted to surround herself with people who wanted more. People who wanted to achieve, compete, and feel the reward of their labor.

We started discussing different career paths for her and what courses she might want to take to pursue them. She seriously considered going back for a Master's Degree in Hospitality. She also considered taking a sommelier course and earning her certification. She had always been a bit concerned about working in the restaurant industry, which often pays the most money for working night (dinner) shifts. She has told me many times that she doesn't think that is a sustainable lifestyle choice for her and wouldn't be great for work vs. home balance.

Then she said what she really wanted was a job that was well-respected, where she could wear a suit every day, work mostly during the day, and make a lot of money to support her family.

I had to break the bad news to her. "Sealy, it sounds like you want to be a lawyer." She laughed and agreed.

We had discussed law school many times over the years, and she had gone as far as taking the LSAT once. But having been through law school myself, I told her back then I didn't think she was ready. I told her I didn't think her emotional maturity was ready for the brutal beast that is law school. We both agree that she has grown a lot through the ups and downs of her jobs since college, though. I now believe she is in a good space to be like one of those "more mature" law students I witnessed who had worked in another field before law school. These were the students who had the maturity to stay in the library all day between classes and treat it as a job.

So, as of this writing, she is preparing to take the LSAT again in hopes to raise her score. She has completed a month-long course where, in addition to class time, she has created and followed a thirty-five-hour per week study plan—in addition to working at the restaurant on Fridays, Saturdays, and Sundays. Receiving this schedule alone was a great coup and the result of having exceeded expectations at work. We will see where this chapter takes her. The road of the restart just keeps meandering along.

CHAPTER 12

═══

WES STARTS OVER, TOO!

I like to think the reason I didn't finish this book two years ago when I *should* have is so that I could share this newly unfolding restart with you. I hope it brings home the point that if you are open to developing a richer, more beautiful life, doors to new restarts will never stop opening for you.

I have told you that Wes is a naturally talented artist. He has drawn, created, and sculpted his entire life. He clearly inherited the talent from his mother, who is incredibly gifted in her own right. One of my favorite pieces of Wes's artwork was done when he was only six years old. He colored a bottle of soda with two pieces of fruit in front of it. The amazing thing was how the bottle actually looked clear, and you could see the dimension in the pitted cork in the bottle's mouth. In front of the bottle were two pieces of fruit, clearly showing depth with one in front of the other. This was not the coloring project of a normal six-year-old.

I think most artistic talent comes with drawbacks. Wes is highly dyslexic, which makes reading very challenging for him, although he forces himself to push through it. It makes sense to me that someone who sees words on the page differently might also see depth, shadow, and color differently, as well. I believe a challenge usually has a silver lining. His silver lining is definitely the way he sees beauty in the world, and the way he can put that vision onto paper or carve it into a sculpture.

A few months ago, while flying home from a European cruise, I got a wild hair during some boring airplane time and thought I should try to find an art course for Wes. Not a little one-week course, but something more intense, more exotic. Something in Florence, Italy! Where else would one go abroad to study art? I found the city had several schools, so I started researching which would be best for him. I came across the Accademia D'Arte which is an old style bottega or workshop where students learn alongside the masters, just the way Leonardo and Michelangelo did in this same town 500 years ago. They offered courses for as many weeks as you wanted, with a new class starting every Monday.

So, we went all-out and signed him up for a month-long course during the month of September. Naturally, we had never been apart like this; but we decided it would be worth it. Of course, I could technically have gone with him, but I believed the most important part of the course was giving him a full, *undistracted* month of working on his art, with nothing else tugging at him. We packed him up and sent him off to a short-term rental for the month. I knew that when it was over, he would want to introduce me to the people he had met and take me to the restaurants he had discovered, so I planned to arrive on the day his course ended. I would spend ten days visiting Florence with him, as well as a few surrounding Tuscan towns.

From the beginning of the course, he excelled. All of us back home were astounded at the images he was sending us. They began the course by painting in oil a replica of Dante's muse, *Beatrice*, by William Dyce. As he began copying the painting, his instructors began to take serious note of his skill. I knew he was talented, but even I wasn't aware of just how good he really is. If one big leap of faith weren't enough, we were about to be thrown another curveball!

Two weeks into the four-week course, the head of the school pulled a chair up beside Wes and asked him, "How committed are you?" Wes said, "Well, I mean I came all the way to Italy!" The instructor then told him that, based on his work, they recommended that he move to the Masters course. He told Wes about all the great things he would learn there, including additional old-world techniques for mixing paint, sculpting, and drawing. Apparently, one student who had applied for that program and turned in a full portfolio had not been able to come. There was room for one more person now, and the program had just started that very day.

Wes thought this all sounded exciting, so he asked how long it would last. Nine months was the disappointing answer. Students in the program receive a Masters in Visual Arts, so the curriculum is scheduled throughout a typical school year from September through May.

On our daily call, Wes relayed the story to me, laughing when he got to the part about nine months. I laughed, too. We had never been apart for even a week! Then I saw Savannah and showed her his latest work and told her about the offer. Of course, I was laughing like it was a bit pie-in-the-sky. Without missing a beat, she said, "What do you mean? *Of course* he should do it. You have the ability to go visit him, and he'll be home for a month at Christmas."

She was right. What were we thinking? Of course he should do it! I was capable of holding down the fort at home, and this was an amazing—and very unexpected—opportunity for him. So I texted him: "I think you should do it." His response was along the lines of, "What? We really need to talk about this." And so we did; and that very day, we realized that we were being shortsighted, and this was an incredible opportunity that shouldn't be passed up.

So, while Wes was painting and sculpting and moving over into the other program, my work began. I set about working on all the drudgery of getting his student visa approved. He didn't need one for a thirty-day course, but he certainly did for a full school year! I also had to find a new place for him to live, because the place he had been staying wasn't available for this new extended stay. I decided to visit him at the end of thirty days as planned but extended my stay a few days to be able to help him move to the new place and get him settled in for the long haul. I'm actually finishing this final book edit in Florence while he is in class.

This strange turn of events has given me something of an epiphany. If it hadn't unfolded in just this way, it wouldn't have happened at all. I never would have thought to look for a full school-year program, since it wouldn't have occurred to me that we could be apart that long. Even if I had looked for one and found it, he would have laughed. I don't think there is any way he would have agreed to go. But since he came for a month and was succeeding, his confidence level was high. It was not nearly as scary to take the next step to agree to stay.

This is what keeping doors open in our lives, and having the courage to walk through them, can do. This is the beautiful tapestry of life that is only visible after we have walked through the open doors. It takes courage and faith, but it's the only path to true self-actualization. What will Wes do with his art? With his talent? We can't know that yet. But we are at peace. We know we have made the best choice for his life and that doors will continue to open because he had the fortitude to step through this first one. What incredible door could be open to you if you're willing to take that first step?

CONCLUSION

I have a friend who is a successful realtor—sixty-five years old, thin, fit, never smoked a day in her life—and she posted on Facebook that she has lung cancer. She has been fighting it for a year, and she thought she had it beat, but she didn't. She was calling in hospice. She had only been married to her new husband for three years. She said, "This was the year I was going to retire! This was the year I was going to spend time with my husband! There's so much I haven't done. Please don't let this be you. Go out and *live*." As of today, she is still fighting valiantly but faces a nearly impossible battle.

Of course, I don't wish this for anyone, but any of us might get that call someday: that you're going on hospice. You're not going to ever retire. You're not traveling anywhere. Everything you worked so hard for is just going to be...over.

I don't want to get that call at sixty-five or ever. But if I do, I'll say, "Thank goodness I've been to fifty countries. I had my babies, married the love of my life, and welcomed his kids into my family, too. Thank goodness I didn't wait until today, the end of my life, when I'm sick and frail and hurting, to try to do something."

There's always that restart we wish for that we never get. We can't act like we'll live forever, so anything you want to do, you have to start doing it now.

Think seriously about what that means for you and for your family.

DIE WITH ZERO

A friend recently told me about a book called *Die With Zero*, by Bill Perkins. My friend said, "You need to read this book. I think you will love it, because I feel like it's the way you guys are already living."

Well, I read it, and it's the most wonderful book. It talks about intentionally spending all your money so you have basically nothing left the day you die. The author says that the person who wins is the one who dies with zero dollars, because that means you extracted every minute of joy from your life. It is exactly with that attitude that we've lived our lives.

People I've told about this idea I'm so passionate about have said, "Oh, I could never do that. Isn't that irresponsible?"

No! It isn't. In fact, I think it's irresponsible to think, "We're going to wait until we're seventy-five to start traveling."

We all get to a certain age where things are more difficult, physically, and where our desire and ability to enjoy traveling and many other experiences goes down. Why wait and save up your whole life and then be too tired to enjoy everything you've worked so hard for?

Instead, you should start enjoying everything you have as early as you can. Don't put it off for later. We're not guaranteed tomorrow.

We recently took a trip to Egypt, and people who saw the pictures on social media said, "Oh my gosh, you just spent a month in Egypt?" We sure did, and it was amazing. Wes and I are fifty-five and fifty-seven, so we can still do it easily. We could climb inside the pyramids, crawling on our hands and knees down a six-hundred-foot tunnel and back. If we had waited fifteen or twenty years, we might not have been able to. At the very least, we likely wouldn't have enjoyed it in the same way. And I have zero guarantee that I'll be here in fifteen or twenty years, so I'm going to do what I can now.

Another question I get after sharing the book's concept is, "What about leaving money for my kids?"

One of the most interesting things the author said in *Die With Zero* is that the average age of inheritance is *sixty years old*. Do you think the amount of money your children stand to inherit will help them more when they're sixty, or when they're twenty-nine and closer to just getting started in the world?

Give what you can, now, to your kids. If they want to buy a home or invest in a business, it will change the trajectory of their life, and you will get the joy of watching them do it. I've always said I don't want my kids to be torn about thinking,

"Boy, I never want Mom to die, but it sure would be nice to have that money."

Of course, you have to be smart about having enough money to take care of your expenses. But most people save too much for the end of their lives, because they think they're going to have the same wants and needs. The older and frailer we get, however, the less we want and need, and the less we are able to do.

My mom died with around six thousand dollars to her name because she had given my brother and me everything she had as we went along. I always made sure she had enough money to live comfortably, and she enjoyed seeing me build the business. She got to see and enjoy all of it.

By contrast, I know a man who recently died of cancer in his late eighties. He asked all his kids to come visit him to talk about the will and what he was leaving them. Ironically, by the time they all arrived, he was too sick to visit much. But regardless of that, in my mind, he waited too long! He was eighty-seven, and his kids are from their late fifties to early sixties. He chose to wait until his wife dies for the children to inherit, to make sure their mother is taken care of. That seems noble, but we're talking about more money than one person— especially a modest, conservative person like her—will ever spend toward the end of her life. She already has everything she needs, and if the parents' desire for all that money was to help their three children, they should have already done that. They should have done it while the kids could have made the most of the financial help and while the parents were alive and healthy enough to enjoy seeing their children experience financial freedom.

It's all about living and giving.

Just like with your kids, if you have a charity you care about, don't leave your money to them after you die. Give it to them now. They need it and can use it today.

I'm going to do my best to die with zero, to the extent that I can, and I'm going to enjoy every minute God blesses me with. What's more, not only am I going to be able to help my children financially, but I'm also going to do whatever I can to be here to give them guidance in the meanwhile. That gives more meaning to my money and my life.

BETTER THAN EVER

My life is better now than I ever could have dreamed.

In fact, I wish I could go back to that twenty-three-year-old girl who thought her life was over when her husband decided to leave and show her a snapshot of the life she would be living today. I am married to a caring, giving man who genuinely loves me. He even brought along some added bonuses. Can you imagine the blessing that Wes's children, now all grown and beginning to marry, as well, have been to me? Once the mother of two, I find myself with five very unique, talented, diverse, wise children—and I couldn't be happier.

If I hadn't been through the challenges and painful experiences from my past, I wouldn't have Chase, Bridger, and Lexi in my life. And that is simply unthinkable at this point.

Isn't it amazing the good things that God can bring out of our own failures and disappointments? These three wonderful people have been among the greatest bonuses of my life, and I love them dearly.

I want to be able to pass these ideas on to the next generation. And I want people in the next generation, whether that's any of my children, or the young people I talk with, or you reading this book, to learn from my experiences. I hope that very few bad things ever happen to you. But life is a winding road with lots of paths and detours. Hardly any of us make it straight through on the road we start out on, so don't be shocked or upset by that.

Embrace and learn to love the restart right from day one, so you can see it for the blessing it is and turn it into an intentional change for the better on your journey.

YOU GOTTA HAVE HOPE

Finally, and most of all, I want you to have *hope*.

When you're in the middle of a new restart, which likely means something not-so-great has happened, you need hope. When you hear people's stories and they say, "I made it through that. It stunk, but guess what? I'm so happy now," it makes you feel like maybe you're going to be fine, too. You need to keep seeing that end result and reminding yourself that we've all been through these hard times, but they end eventually and often leave us better than before—with the knowledge that there's (almost) always going to be another restart.

If you're in a place where things are going pretty good at the moment, then I want to motivate you to analyze your life. Is it enough? Are you getting what you need? Are you giving to others what you can? Have you gotten a little complacent?

But if you're in the middle of a painful restart, and you're just not sure you can make it through, I want more than anything for you to have hope that it is absolutely going to be okay. *You* are going to be okay. You'll get through this.

Remember that whichever of these two places you're in now, you will be in the other place at some point—in the next month, next year, or five years from now. We are all destined to live in both of those places. Just know that you may need to go back and read this book again when you're in the other phase, because you'll get something different out of it—hope, inspiration, and the knowledge that you have what it takes not just to survive this life but to make your own restart and live life better than ever before.

I hope you have found something useful in this book, to make your life a little better, change your mindset, or increase your level of happiness.

While I certainly don't have all the answers to all of life's challenges, for me, the ultimate victory is never giving up. If you aren't happy in your career, change it. If you don't like your appearance, work on it. If you aren't happy in your marriage, do everything in your power to fix it. If you are with someone who doesn't want to fix it, then you have some tough decisions to make. Nothing says you have to wait around for the next restart to come along. You have the tools to *create* the next restart in your own life!

Despite being in a really good place, we are actively looking into opening a restaurant, something I thought I would never do. At fifty-five, I am still excited about and—and more capable of—starting new businesses and opening new chapters. Restarting is not a one-and-done. It's a muscle you build over time that can bring a lot of happiness, confidence, and peace into your life.

Promise me one thing: that you will ask *yourself*, "Is this *it* for me?" And listen to your heart's honest answer.

If you aren't living your best, happiest life, promise me you'll take the risk, do the work, give your one at-bat in life *all* you have! After all, until we meet on the other side in Glory, it *is* all you have. Don't waste it.

ACKNOWLEDGMENTS

I want to thank my wonderful husband Wes for loving me when I'm unlovable, for looking at me with the sweetest, most loving eyes I've ever seen, and for truly believing in his core that I hung the moon. Having the privilege of spending these years with you has been, and I know will continue to be, one of the most beautiful blessings of my life. I love you forever!

And to my two daughters, who have been with me the longest—I suppose you were inside me when I was born, and you are with me today. To the two girls who have taught me more than I could ever hope to have taught them: you are my legacy, my greatest gift to this world. I love you both so much!

I want to thank my mother in heaven once again for being my biggest supporter always, for teaching me right from wrong, and for giving me the tools to take on any situation with courage and with grace. There will never be another Jeannine Jordan. I owe you everything, Mom!

ABOUT THE AUTHOR

After graduating from the University of Texas Law School in 1990 and practicing as a trial lawyer for five years, Tammy moved to Fredericksburg, Texas, in 1995 and began opening retail boutiques. In 2001, she moved, unwittingly, into the vacation rental space when she renovated a 1910 Victorian carriage house on the grounds of her home and then decided to rent it out as a B&B.

In 2007, she opened Absolute Charm B&Bs and Vacation Rentals, Fredericksburg's premier luxury reservation service, which now represents around 200 properties. Over the years, she has bought, renovated, and sold twenty-five vacation rental properties of her own.

In 2015, Tammy and her husband, Wes Pack, opened Absolute Charm Real Estate; with the help of their great team, they grew the company into the number one office in Fredericksburg, Texas, by volume in less than four years. In 2018, they moved their team to eXp Realty as a Mega Team. In 2021, the team sold more volume than any other team at eXp Realty with ten to twenty agents.

Tammy has spoken on "the big stage" regarding a diverse area of topics, including real estate marketing, using social media and personal branding, leadership, and sales skills. In August of 2017, she spoke at Tom Ferry's Success Summit in front of six thousand realtors in the live audience and more than thirty thousand watching the live stream. Her YouTube video from that event has been viewed over 400,000 times and counting. That engagement led to her being paid to fly to London to speak at the Spicerhaart Summit in front of 800 "estate agents," as they are known in the UK, on building a personal brand by delivering top-notch service and hospitality. She also spoke to over four thousand agents in 2022 at the Build22 Event in Dallas on why agents need to invest more of their personal money in real estate and how they could do so using creative financing.

Tammy enjoys spending time with her husband, Wes, and their two white Persian cats, Coco and Frank. Coco has quite the social media following on Instagram (@princesscocobeans), and the two of them provide endless entertainment! Tammy also enjoys traveling with Wes and as many of their five grown children as they can wrangle up at any given time. She and Wes spend as much time as they can at their second home in Natchez, Mississippi, where they have made so many wonderful friends who are now like family.